WRITING LAB

Grades 4-7

W9-BFN-007

DL 69

Clarity
Fluency
Revision
Persuasive Writing
Descriptive Writing
and more

Written by **Nancy Atlee**
Illustrated by **Mary Lou Johnson**
and **Annelise Palouda**

Edited by **Dianne Draze**

ISBN 0-931724-88-0

Contents

Introduction

What Is a Writing Lab?

An hour a week is all it takes to create a learning laboratory where everyone enjoys writing. The *Writing Lab* helps promote fluency in writing while simultaneously developing students' abilities in all phases of the writing process. The laboratory setting creates an experimental, risk-free learning environment where students develop and hone their writing skills. This is a comprehensive supplement to the writing curriculum, not a substitute for it. The *Writing Lab* is based on recognition of the following:

- writing is intrinsically related to thinking and oral communication skills
- not all students excel or are fluent in writing
- students benefit from instruction in effective writing skills
- students benefit from risk-free opportunities to practice and develop skills
- not all student work needs to be evaluated by a teacher
- writing is fun.

Why Write?

Writing is the ultimate communication skill. It requires clear thinking and the ability to express thoughts by using language effectively. In a very real sense, writing defines an individual in both business and personal settings.

Teaching students how to write effectively is essential. Yet, once the stages of the writing process are taught, many teachers find it difficult to maintain an instructional program that continues to develop student writing skills. The emphasis shifts toward "doing" various writing assignments and away from "how to do" different kinds of writing.

For the Busy Teacher

The *Writing Lab* gives students a great deal of practice in writing without generating additional paperwork for busy teachers. Lab lessons are enabling exercises. Each lesson is a finite instructional experience. Teacher and students work together during the class period. When the lab is over, papers are filed in students' writing folders. Those who are absent are not required to make up the lab lesson.

The *Writing Lab* keeps teacher preparation and work at a minimum. The first page of each section explains the rationale and contents of the section. The purpose and objectives of each lesson are clearly stated on student worksheets. No additional materials or preparation are necessary. The instructor need only be an active participant in the lesson.

Student worksheets include a presentation of the concept and instruction, examples that illustrate the concept, partner writing exercises, and finally individual writing exercises. Evaluation of student lab work is informal. The teacher's active involvement in the lab and oral sharing of work constitute formative evaluation during the lesson itself. Student writing folders provide a continuous record of student lab work and may be reviewed whenever necessary.

Student Outcomes

Teachers who use activities from *Writing Lab* find significant student improvement in several areas. Students become more fluent writers. They develop and support their ideas more effectively and include more elaboration in their language arts and social studies assignments. Secondly, students demonstrate greater ability to vary their writing. Thirdly, students benefit from consistent practice in the revision stage of the writing process. Though the specific focus of each lab may vary, students are continuously revising and reworking written material to make it more effective. The net result is **students become better writers**.

Classroom Set-up

Time Scheduling

Schedule a regular time for the writing lab, usually 45-60 minutes per week. The lab can either be used as an integral part of the regular language arts block or as an additional instructional period.

Make Draft Folders

Give each student a manila file folder for all rough drafts and lab work. Reproduce the following reference sheets (one per student) and staple them to the inside covers of the draft folders:

- The Writing Process (page 8)
- Domains of Writing (page 9)
- Editing (page 10)
- Rules for Correct Writing (page 11)

Discuss each reference sheet. Be sure students are familiar with the content and guidelines of each sheet. Point out that they can use these reference sheets during lab activities or when working on drafts of more formal writing assignments. Keep all student folders in a box that is readily accessible.

Make Portfolio Folders

Create a writing folder to hold each student's final drafts of full-process assignments. Distinguish portfolios from draft folders by having students illustrate the covers or decorate them with gift wrap paper. Keep folders where they can be easily seen by class visitors.

Using the Writing Lab Materials

Select a lab lesson and duplicate student worksheets. Because lessons within each section are developmental rather than sequential, teachers can select from any section. It is not necessary to teach every lesson in a section.

A lesson is designed to stand alone so teachers can structure the writing lab to meet the needs of students. When lab lessons are taught on a rotating basis, student interest remains high.

A schedule for the first seven labs might look like this:

Week 1 - Fluency Lesson 1
Week 2 - Fluency Lesson 2
Week 3 - Descriptive Writing Lesson 1
Week 4 - Sentence Lesson 3
Week 5 - Fluency Lesson 3
Week 6 - Clarity Lesson 1
Week 7 - Paragraph Lesson 1

Note: Once a fluency technique is taught as a lesson, it is used (without a student worksheet) as a writing warm-up exercise.

Teacher Modeling

Model your thinking and writing. Using an overhead projector, write with students so they can watch you work and revise. Teacher modeling is essential during fluency warm-ups and the first exercise(s) of each lab lesson. It is important that students see you use the writing process, modifying ideas and experimenting with words, phrases, and organizational structure.

These are examples of some things you might say to elicit student input:

"This word/phrase doesn't seem to fit here. I need to revise the passage with a synonym or reword it. Help me with this problem."

"I need a word here that starts with r. Any suggestions?"

"I was stuck on this passage until I decided to turn it into a quotation."

Teacher modeling also helps slow or reluctant writers get started. By following your example or even copying your work, these students become immediately involved in the lesson, thus ensuring whole class participation. Fluent student writers tend to proceed on their own, but they also like to discuss your writing problems and help you solve them.

Creating a Risk-Free Environment

Keep the feeling of the lab spontaneous. Help students see that writing can be fun. Write along with your students. Accept divergent responses to fluency exercises. Encourage students to take risks and experiment with ideas and language.

Have students work in small groups. Writing with partners gives them an opportunity to discuss different approaches to writing problems and to explore possible solutions. Sharing writing with other members of the group also helps develop an appreciation of the richness of language and the variety of writing styles.

Model Lesson Plan

A writing lab lesson consists of three parts. Planning time is minimal. Simply select the fluency exercise and instructional lesson for the day and duplicate student worksheets.

Opening (15 minutes)

This period is designed to involve all students in writing immediately, prevent writer's block, and create a risk-free atmosphere for enjoyment and experimentation. Follow this procedure:

1. Have students get draft folders, pencils and paper.
2. Begin with a fluency warm-up exercise to get everyone thinking and writing.
3. Share ideas from the fluency exercise by reading to partners, table read-arounds, or oral reading to the entire class. Discuss any problem-solving strategies that were used.

Lab Lesson of the Day (20-35 minutes)

This is the instructional part of the writing lab. During this time a specific writing skill or process is introduced, practiced or extended. This is the usual procedure for this part of the lab time:

1. Read and discuss the focus of the specific lesson (descriptive or persuasive writing, clarity, paragraph development, etc.).
2. Discuss the writing problem (specialized vocabulary, sentence structure, organization, clarity, etc.) and possible solutions as shown in the examples.
3. Write with a partner, then individually. When working with a partner, it is important that both students write. They may share ideas, but they should each produce a writing sample. Then each student will develop their own ideas in an individual writing sample.
4. Share and discuss written work at the end of this period.

Closing (10 minutes)

The last section of the lab is used to focus on the practical applications of the lab lesson. The procedure is as follows:

1. Share examples of student work, noting the various writing strategies students used in the instructional lesson.
2. Discuss curricular areas where students can apply the strategies of the instructional lesson; for instance, responses to reading and social studies, writing clearer test answers, creating a clearer sequence of events, more effective revisions on full-process lessons, making writing more descriptive, writing a better summary, organizing a research report, persuading a reader.
3. Have students place all lab work in their draft folders and replace the folders in the box.

File this in your writing folder for reference.

The Writing Process

In order to be an effective writer, a person needs two things — something meaningful to say and the writing skills to say it clearly.

Steps in the Writing Process

Prewriting

1. Collect ideas, cluster, brainstorm and take notes.
2. Organize ideas into main topics and arrange ideas into a basic, overall structure. Decide on the point of view and style.

Writing

3. Write a rough draft. Get ideas down on paper. Don't worry about spelling or grammar. If possible, put the piece aside for a day or more.
4. Reread, rethink, revise. This is one of the most important steps in the process. Rethink the purpose and the content of the written piece. As you read the work, pretend you are seeing it for the first time and know nothing about what the author is trying to say. Elaborate ideas or delete repetitive material. You might decide to change the point of view. Pay attention to paragraph organization and clarity of ideas. Look at sentence structure, variety and style. Make needed revisions and write a second draft.

Polishing

5. Edit the work. Correct spelling, grammar and punctuation.
6. Put the written piece in the final form. Add a title page, table of contents, bibliography, or any other supplementary material.

When Time Is a Factor

Working through the entire process takes time. Essay tests and overnight assignments limit the amount of time a writer has. However, even when time is short, do not eliminate steps one through five. Rather, you should adjust the amount of time you give to each part of the writing process.

Domains of Writing

There are four main categories of writing called domains. The writer's purpose for writing helps him or her decide what domain (style of writing) to use. Each domain has certain characteristics. The chart below explains each of the four domains of writing.

Sensory/Descriptive
Purpose: entertain the reader, use vivid detail and language, create a visual image, express individual feelings

Characteristics: descriptive language appeals to the five senses; imagery, simile, metaphor, personification, adjectives and adverbs, first or third person point of view

Examples: personal narrative, personal memoir, journal, diary, friendly letter, personal essay, poem

Practical/Informative
Purpose: inform the reader, present factual information clearly

Characteristics: factual, main ideas supported by specific examples, logical organization and sequence of ideas, third person point of view

Examples: research report, directions, newspaper article, business letter, summary, encyclopedia article, textbook chapter, memo, research or lecture notes

Narrative/Imaginative
Purpose: entertain the reader, relate an event within a time sequence (factual or fiction)

Characteristics: logical sequence of events, rising action leading to a climax, possible use of flashback, first or third person point of view

Examples: short story, novel, fable, myth, folk tale, tall tale, epic poem, reader's theater script

Analytical/Expository
Purpose: explain information, analyze information, or persuade the reader

Characteristics: reflects research, analytical thinking and/or evaluation, clear language, logical organization, third person point of view

Examples: compare/contrast essay, persuasive essay or paragraph, character analysis, literary analysis, book report, political or persuasive speech, editorial, letter to the editor, movie or book review

Editing

Writers edit their work after content revisions have been made. The editing requires slow, deliberate examination of written material. Writers and editors use symbols to mark the kinds of corrections made during the editing process. Student writers use these same symbols. The following list contains the most commonly used editing marks.

Editing Marks

Editing Mark	Meaning	Example
≡	Capitalize	houston, texas
/	Lower case letter	my ¢at
⊙	Add a period	I went to town⊙
⋏	Add a comma	apples, oranges⋏and grapes
ⱽ ⱽ	Add quotation marks	ⱽWatch out! he called:
ⱽ	Add apostrophe	He wonⱽt come.
∧	Add something	It belongs∧to me. Dear Sir∧
e	Delete something	Give it it to her.
———	Correct spelling	imagination ~~immagination~~
———	Correct a word	he had ~~blew~~ out the candle (blown)
₣	Indent paragraph	₣ My first experience...
⌐	Reverse word order or letter order	luck good, teh

Rules for Correct Writing

Capitalization

Use a **capital letter** for the following:

- first word of a sentence
- first and last names of people
- names of specific places (streets, cities, states, countries, oceans, mountains, rivers and planets)
- names of specific businesses, organizations and nationalities
- names of days, months, and specific holidays
- greeting and closing of letters
- the pronoun "I"
- first word and other important words in titles of books, stories, plays, movies, poems and songs
- the first word of a direct quotation.

Punctuation

Use a **period:**

- at the end of a statement or request
- after an initial or an abbreviation.

Use a **comma:**

- between words or phrases in a series
- after the day, when a date is written using month, day and year
- between the street, city, and state when it appears in the middle of a sentence
- before a conjunction (and, but, yet, for, or, nor) that divides a compound sentence
- after yes, no, a noun of address, and interjections that begin a sentence
- after the greeting in a friendly letter
- after the closing in business and friendly letters
- around appositive phrases — *Mark, the first baseman, came to the plate.*
- after a long introductory phrase or subordinate clause that begins a sentence *When I think of pickles, my mouth begins to water.*
- before or after direct quotations.

Rules for Correct Writing, continued

Use a **question mark** at the end of a question.

Use an **exclamation point** at the end of a sentence that shows strong emotion or an urgent command.

Use a **semi-colon** between the two halves of a compound sentence when a conjunction has not been used or when the two clauses are long and contain commas.

Use a **colon:**

- before a list or series of words or ideas
- between the hour and minutes
- after the greeting of a business letter.

Use **quotation marks:**

- around exact words spoken in a direct quotation
- around the titles of short stories, television shows, magazine and newspaper articles, poems, and songs.

Use an **underline** for titles of books, magazines, newspapers, movies, plays, long poems, long musical compositions, works of art and names of ships.

John ordered an ice cream cone; Sarah's selection was a doughnut.

Word Usage

When you write pay attention to:

- noun/verb agreement — *Bob runs. Bob and Carol run.*
- noun/pronoun agreement — *Bob...he; Bob and Carol...they*
- correct use of subject/object pronouns — *He gave the book to her. She took the book.*

Sentence Construction

- eliminate fragments and run-ons
- avoid needless repeated words and phrases by combining sentences
- vary the sentence structure

Paragraph Construction

- develop the paragraph around one main topic or main idea
- indent the first word of the paragraph
- begin a new paragraph for each speaker when writing dialogue

Fluency

Developing Fluent Writers

Fluency is the ability to write smoothly, expressing oneself through writing as easily as speaking. Language, phrasing and sequential development of ideas flow freely from the writer's mind onto the paper. Fluent writers work easily with written language. They state ideas clearly and elaborate by manipulating words and phrases to suit their purpose for writing. They recognize the fact that there is more than one "right" way to state an idea.

The first few words of any assignment are often the most difficult to write. For many students, looking at a blank piece of paper can be intimidating, especially if they lack confidence in their writing skills. We can help these students develop fluency in writing. Just as athletes warm up muscles before using them strenuously to full capacity, students can warm up for writing. Experience shows that putting something on paper helps students avoid a feeling of writer's block.

There are two stages of development in the fluency lessons. The first stage involves writing a specific type of sentence. For example, students write a sentence following a given letter pattern. Then, once students have solved the original problem, the second stage asks them to write another sentence, solving the same problem in a different way. As the year progresses and they develop more fluency, expect students to write three to five sentences in a given pattern.

Fluency Lessons

There are six lessons in this section. These lessons are:

Lesson 1 - Using Letter Patterns
Lesson 2 - Building Sentences
Lesson 3 - Using Sentence Elements
Lesson 4 - Working Backwards
Lesson 5 - Alliteration
Lesson 6 - Brainstorming

Using the Fluency Worksheets

Warm-up exercises promote fluency by involving students in writing immediately, at the very beginning of a lab lesson. The activities are open-ended and often require both creativity and experimentation with language. As they warm up, encourage students to discuss a variety of possible responses with a partner. Encourage them to try different ideas and create several sentences for each exercise. Allow time for sharing work with others in the group or with the entire class.

Familiarize students with the different writing warm-up patterns by teaching each exercise as a separate lesson. Once students have completed a fluency worksheet and know the format, the warm-up activity can be used interchangeably to begin any writing lesson. Create additional fluency exercises by asking students to contribute ideas for practice sentences by varying letters, elements or alliterative sounds.

Evaluation

Evaluation of the fluency worksheets is informal. Ask students to discuss strategies they used to solve the writing problem. Then ask them to place a check by the written response they think is the most effective example of their own writing.

Name _____

Using Letter Patterns

In this exercise you will be writing sentences that have a certain pattern. The words in the following sentences all begin with the same letter pattern.

Letter Pattern — S P Y T D M A C

Sample sentences

Sebastian pays you to dress my aunt's cat.

Students painfully yell to decrease many assignments constantly.

So, Peggy, you took Dad's money after class.

The writer had to solve the writing problem by thinking about the letters in a different way for each sentence. Some of the sentences are written more effectively than others. Underline the sentence you think makes the clearest statement. Be prepared to give a reason for your answer.

 **Work With A Partner**

Use the following letter patterns to write sentences. Begin each word in the sentence with a letter from the pattern. Follow the letter sequence exactly as it is given with no additions or deletions. When you are finished put a * by the sentence you think makes the clearest statement.

Letter pattern - M W G A C T P

1._____

2._____

Work With A Partner

Letter pattern - J H A B T T R

1. _____

2. _____

Letter pattern - W L A F T O P J

1. _____

2. _____

On Your Own

Write sentences using each letter pattern. When you are finished, put a * by the sentence you think makes the clearest statement.

Letter pattern - W D Y S T H F C

1. _____

2. _____

Letter pattern - T R F E S D T H

1. _____

2. _____

Create your own letter pattern. Use it to write two sentences.

Letter pattern _____

1. _____

2. _____

Name _____

Building Sentences

In this exercise you will be trying to write sentences that have a certain number of words and deal with a specific topic. Here are examples of five-word sentences on the topic of homework, six-word sentences on the topic of sports and seven-word sentences on the topic of politics.

5 words - *I don't particularly like homework.*
           Homework is the worst torture.

6 words - *Playing baseball is a favorite pastime.*
           Tom, which sport is your favorite?

7 words - *Harold was elected as our class president.*
           We elect our President every four years.

 **Work With A Partner**

Use the following topics to write two sentences containing the exact number of words shown.

5 words - *friends* _____

_____

6 words - *space* _____

_____

✏️ Work With A Partner ✏️

7 words - *baseball* _____

_____

8 words - *movies* _____

_____

9 words - *ice cream* _____

_____

10 words - *fads* _____

_____

On Your Own

Write two sentences for each of these topics.

5 words - *pets* _____

_____

6 words - *science* _____

_____

7 words - *books* _____

_____

8 words - *vacations* _____

_____

9 words - *fast foods* _____

_____

10 words - *airplanes* _____

_____

Name _____

Using Sentence Elements

Like a story, a sentence has three elements — characters, setting, and plot or idea. You combine these elements to write a sentence. When you combine the same elements in different ways, the meaning of the sentences can change. In the following example, one set of elements has been used to create two different sentences.

Elements

winter   taxi driver
frequently   naturalist
Agent 0009

Sample Sentences

During the cold winter, Agent 0009 frequently disguises himself as a naturalist or a taxi driver.

Agent 0009, dressed as a taxi driver, was hired to follow the naturalist who was traveling to Europe for a winter vacation.

✏️ Work With A Partner ✏️

Use the following sets of elements to write a sentence. When you have completed one sentence, think about the elements in a different way. Then write another sentence.

Elements

skateboard   model   suddenly
beach   doctor   bicycle

1. _____

2. _____

 **Work With A Partner**

Elements

painter	plane	never
Paris	map	dog

1. _____

2. _____

On Your Own

Use these elements to write a pair of sentences. Try to make each sentence express a different idea.

Elements

actor	Wednesday	writer
New York	stunt man	soon

1. _____

2. _____

Create your own set of elements. Use it to write two sentences.

_____	_____	_____
(proper noun)	(city)	(month)
_____	_____	_____
(occupation)	(mode of travel)	(adverb)

1. _____

2. _____

Read the sentences you have written. Mark the sentence that makes the clearest statement.

Name _____

Working Backwards

Writers sometimes have a difficult time getting started. The first few sentences seem to be the hardest to write. One way to avoid this problem is to start with an ending and work backwards. Using this technique, it is the writer's job to create a situation that leads to that ending.

Example:

Ending - ***Three times around the kingdom did it!***

George, the dragon-slayer, was out of shape. It was getting harder and harder to chase down a raging beast and slay it. The king was showing displeasure by threatening to banish George from the kingdom. He consulted the wise man for advice. He asked the magician for a spell. But nothing helped. George started taking long walks into the country. Eventually he began jogging. The jogging eventually built up his strength and endurance. Before long, George had reclaimed his position as head dragon-slayer. When asked for the secret of his recent success, George simply replied, ***"Three times around the kingdom did it!"***

Use the following endings for the work you will do with your partner and the work you will do on your own.

- They all agreed it was the best excuse they had ever heard.
- He knew this had been his last chance.
- No one who had seen that game would ever forget it.
- It was a secret she never wanted repeated.
- They turned the key in the lock and walked away forever.
- Who knows what will wash up on shore during the next storm?
- As she looked at the plans, she realized her invention could change the world.
- "Wow," John exclaimed, "that never occurred to me!"
- Twenty - four plus one was written on the wall.

Work With A Partner

Select one of the suggested endings. Discuss a story line that will lead to the ending. Then write your story on the lines below.

_____

_____

_____

_____

_____

_____

_____

_____

On Your Own

Choose another ending from the list. Use your own ideas to create a situation that leads to the ending. Write your story on the lines below.

_____

_____

_____

_____

_____

_____

_____

_____

_____

Alliteration

Writers work with words and phrases to create different effects. Sometimes when writers choose words for sound or rhythm they repeat a sound over and over. This technique is called alliteration. Here are three examples of alliterative sentences.

· *Behold the big brown boxcars bearing bread baked by Betty.*
· *Kitty-cat capers on the keys, catching my ear with her song.*
· *Clara's constant crying caused Kathy to complain.*

Writers use alliteration both in poetry and prose in a more limited manner than these examples. They experiment with vocabulary until they find a combination of words and sounds that create the intended image. By practicing writing sentences that have many alliterative elements, you will be better able to use smaller alliterative elements in your writing.

✏ **Work With A Partner** ✏

Use the following consonant sounds to write a pair of alliteration sentences for each letter. Try to write sentences in which most of the words begin with the given letter or the letter sound.

S _____

_____

S _____

_____

With A Partner

M _____

_____

M _____

_____

R _____

_____

R _____

_____

Choose one of the topics below. Write a poem that contains alliteration on your chosen topic.

snakes   stairs   food   time

_____

_____

_____

_____

_____

_____

_____

_____

On Your Own

Choose four consonants from your first and last names. Write two alliterative sentences for each letter.

letters

_____   _____

           _____

_____   _____

           _____

_____   _____

           _____

_____   _____

           _____

Be prepared to discuss how you worked with words and sounds to compose your sentences. What problems did you have? How did you solve them?

Name_____

Brainstorming

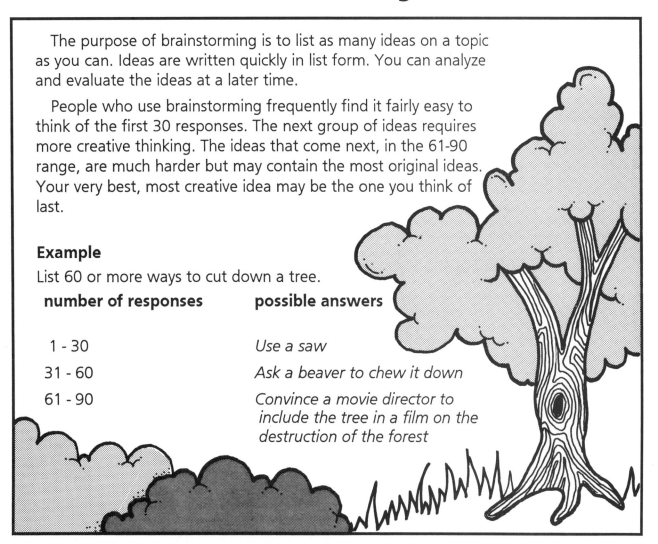

The purpose of brainstorming is to list as many ideas on a topic as you can. Ideas are written quickly in list form. You can analyze and evaluate the ideas at a later time.

People who use brainstorming frequently find it fairly easy to think of the first 30 responses. The next group of ideas requires more creative thinking. The ideas that come next, in the 61-90 range, are much harder but may contain the most original ideas. Your very best, most creative idea may be the one you think of last.

Example

List 60 or more ways to cut down a tree.

number of responses	possible answers
1 - 30	Use a saw
31 - 60	Ask a beaver to chew it down
61 - 90	Convince a movie director to include the tree in a film on the destruction of the forest

➤ **Work With A Partner** ◄

Brainstorm a list of 40-60 (or more) ideas on one of the topics below. When you are finished, mark the five most original ideas on your list.

- *List 40 or more ways to stop a wild animal that is charging right at you.*
- *List 40 or more ways to get to school.*
- *List 40 or more things you can do with an egg.*

1. _____ 2. _____

3. _____ 4. _____

5. _____ 6. _____

Work With A Partner

7. _____   8. _____

9. _____   10. _____

11. _____   12. _____

13. _____   14. _____

15. _____   16. _____

17. _____   18. _____

19. _____   20. _____

21. _____   22. _____

23. _____   24. _____

25. _____   26. _____

27. _____   28. _____

29. _____   30. _____

31. _____   32. _____

33. _____   34. _____

35. _____   36. _____

37. _____   38. _____

39. _____   40. _____

On Your Own

Think about the brainstorming process. Be prepared to discuss the thinking skills you used to write your list. How many responses came quickly? Which ideas started a group of related ideas? Did hearing other people's ideas help you add to your list? Compare your thinking patterns at the beginning of the brainstorming session to those you used at the end.

Clarity

Clarity — What It Is and Isn't

Writers use words to express ideas so the readers can recreate the ideas. When writing is effective, the readers follow the writer's train of thought. The readers understand concepts and the sequence of events. They visualize what the writer intends them to "see." They can follow the writer's logical position on an issue. When readers can understand what has been written, the written piece has clarity. Clarity is an essential element of effective writing.

When concepts and ideas are not clearly written, the reader's understanding is compromised. Lack of clarity in writing is caused by:

- awkward word order or phrasing
- confusing sequence of ideas
- repeated wording
- incorrect vocabulary
- agreement problems (noun/pronoun or noun/verb)
- inconsistent verb tense
- inappropriate writing style
- muddled, unclear thinking.

Most student writers exhibit some form(s) of clarity problems. These problems commonly occur when students work in the prewriting and drafting stages of the writing process, as their attention is given to generating ideas and fluency. Sometimes clarity problems occur when students try to rephrase information used from another source. Clarity problems should be solved during the revision stage of the writing process.

Developing Clear Writing Skills

There are two stages in helping students learn to write clearly. First, students must develop an awareness of the concept of clarity in writing. In the clarity lessons, students are asked to look at numerous examples of clarity problems and effective solutions. They are given specific vocabulary to use in identifying, discussing, and correcting the problems.

In the second stage, students are asked to work with sentences that contain clarity problems. They must analyze the writing, identify the problem, and rewrite the sentences clearly. During this revision process they learn to reword and rephrase. They learn to modify the sequence of events and look for noun/verb consistency and agreement. They also learn to combine common ideas into one sentence and separate run-ons into several sentences.

Students develop problem-solving skills in writing just as they do in mathematics. They must analyze the language problem, consider alternative strategies for revision, and select an effective solution. Encourage students to view their work in this section as solving "clarity problems" rather than correcting errors. They should think of the techniques they learn in this section as problem-solving skills.

Contents

Using the Clarity Worksheets

Lessons in this section should be used sequentially. Lesson One, which introduces the concept of clarity, should be taught fairly early in the school year. It establishes basic strategies students use in revising their writing to achieve clarity. Lessons Two and Three contain more specific examples of clarity problems that commonly occur in student work. These writing exercises are more difficult and require a higher level of analysis and writing skill. They can be used in later writing labs throughout the year as student need arises.

As you introduce the lessons to the class, follow these procedures:

- Encourage students to discuss the importance of clarity in all domains of writing. Stress the responsibility of the writer to communicate clearly to the reader.
- Work with the whole class as you discuss the lesson examples. Ask, what types of problems occur? What techniques are used to solve the problems? What other possible solutions might there be?

- Model the first activity on each worksheet by working through it with the entire class. Continue to work with students until you feel they are comfortable with the exercise and can work on their own.

- Following the whole-class presentation have students work with a partner, sharing ideas and discussing writing problems and alternative solutions as they work. Allow time for students to share their ideas and approaches with others in a larger group or with the entire class.

Evaluation

Evaluation of the clarity writing lessons is informal. There are many acceptable variations for the clarity sentences. Ask each group to select the most effective response for each sentence they write on their own. Read group models to the class. Discuss the characteristics of these student models. Ask, how has the writer solved the clarity problem? What techniques (rewording, rephrasing, changing the sequence, etc.) did the writer use?

Finished worksheets should be placed in students' writing folders.

Content Area Applications

Language Arts: revising first drafts, book reports, full-process compositions, improvement in responses to reading

Social Studies: revising research reports, written responses to reading, use of specific examples

Name_____

Identifying Clarity Problems

A writer wants the reader to understand his ideas clearly. First the writer decides what to say. Then he organizes his ideas so the reader can follow them. The writer chooses words, phrases, and sentences carefully. Finally the writer reviews his work to be sure he presented his ideas clearly so the reader can "see" exactly what the writer meant to say. When a writer leaves out any of these steps, his work may be unclear. Common clarity errors are repeated words, awkward phrasing, or the writer's unclear thinking.

Here are some examples of unclear writing that has been revised so it is clearer.

unclear: *I didn't have the slightest idea of what my friend was saying meant.*

clearer: *I didn't have the slightest idea what my friend meant.*

unclear: *The disadvantages to live in Alaska would be there would be a lot of snow. There would be a lot of snow to shovel. It would be very cold.*

clearer: *Two disadvantages to living in Alaska would be the cold and the great amount of snow you would have to shovel.*

Work With A Partner

Identify the clarity problems in the following examples. Look for repeated words, awkward phrasing, or the writer's unclear thinking. Revise each example so the idea is clear.

1. The Pilgrims were the first settlers of Massachusetts first.

_____

_____

◁═▷ Work With A Partner ◁═▷

2. At night, the Indians were outside of the mission walking to their homes outside the mission.

_____

3. The star player seated in where many other fans awaited him.

_____

4. Until he saw the lion behind him, he thought it was boring, which started to run after him.

_____

_____

On Your Own

Identify the clarity problems. Then rewrite each sentence so the meaning is clearer. You may want to use more than one sentence or combine two ideas into one sentence.

1. When the train was climbing higher and higher, the passengers could see how tall the snow-capped mountains looked like.

_____

_____

2. Unfortunately, they did not have the knowledge to know how to make weapons for war.

_____

_____

3. The next stop on our trip will be the Smithsonian Museum. The Smithsonian Museum is located in Washington D.C.

_____

_____

Name_____

Clarity Problems and Solutions

When writers work on the first drafts of their writings, they concentrate on getting the main ideas down on paper. They know they can clarify the content and style of their work later when they revise and write a second draft.

Here is a listing of the most common clarity problems and solutions.

Problems	**Solutions**
1. unclear words or phrases	use synonyms or reword phrases
2. short choppy sentences with . . . . repeated words or ideas	combine into one sentence
3. words or phrases are out of sequence . .	move words or phrases to a more logical position in the sentence
4. singular or plural agreement	rework nouns and their pronouns
5. verb tense agreement	rework verbs

Here is an example of an unclear sentence and how it can be revised for clarity.

unclear: *The two brothers set off immediately for summer camp, and they were given extra blankets and clothes and money to use on their trip from their parents.*

clearer - *When the two brothers were ready to leave for camp, their parents gave them extra blankets, clothes, and money to use on the trip.*

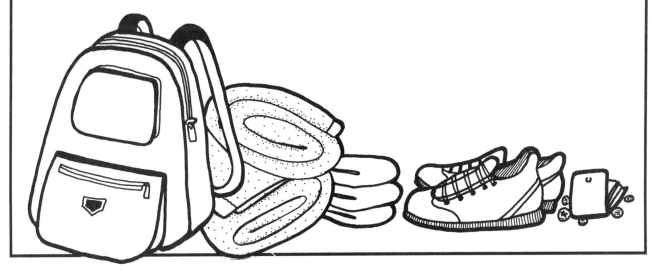

 **Work With A Partner**

Revise the following sentences to make them clearer.

1. The author of the book is Margaret Hodges, and illustrated by Trina Schart Hyman.

2. My brother's bike is from All Sports Store with the hand brakes.

3. Jogging in the bike lane on Main Street, that truck almost hit the runner, I think.

On Your Own

Rewrite each sentence so the meaning is clearer. You may want to use more than one sentence or combine two ideas into one sentence.

1. Bob was able to clean his room garage and washing the car however he doesn't finish mowing the lawn.

2. Hearing the phone ring, the homework was left unfinished by David on the desk.

3. The boy that was the one who took the ball away from the girls was punished. His punishment was that he had to sit against the wall during recess.

Name_____

Clarity Problems in Research Reports

Student writers often incorporate information from various sources in their writing. When they write research reports, they use facts from reference books, textbooks, newspapers and magazines. Sometimes clarity problems occur when they try to state these facts in their own words.

Here are some examples of unclear sentences and how they can be rewritten for clarity.

unclear - *When the Pilgrims hit Plymouth Rock in December, 1620 more people came over the years and Massachusetts became an honorary colony.*

clearer - *The first Pilgrims arrived at Plymouth Rock in December, 1620. Over the next few years, as more and more settlers came, Massachusetts grew into a thriving colony.*

unclear - *Beginning at the Gulf of Mexico, west coast of Florida, and extending west to Mississippi and north to southern Illinois, the East Coastal Plain has two main sections.*

clearer - *The East Coastal Plain has two main sections. It extends west from the Atlantic coast of Florida to Mississippi, and north from the Gulf of Mexico to southern Illinois.*

Inappropriate vocabulary, awkward sequences, and style errors can occur when you rephrase research information for reports. You can solve clarity problems of this kind during the revision stage of the writing process.

 **Work With A Partner**

Revise the following sentences.

1. Throughout the 1600s, there were few important events for about a century.

_____

_____

2. Caused by a warm and sunny climate, Arizona is rich in natural resources. These resources provide Arizona with the advantage of a prosperous economy.

_____

_____

On Your Own

Revise the following sentences. You may decide to use more than one sentence to clarify the meaning or to combine two ideas into one sentence.

1. Followed by the entering of the American trappers, the settlement of the valley was made.

_____

2. There were many first settlers, including the Algonquin Indians, who were there about 3000 years ago, and the Pilgrims, who landed in 1620.

_____

_____

3. Water is the most important resource in Arizona. A reason for this is that so little rain falls in Arizona.

_____

_____

4. An important problem in New York is that is to provide an adequate supply for all the cities in the state and conservation the water at the same time.

_____

_____

Sentences

Sentences are the building blocks of writing. Beginning writers tend to use the same noun-verb-noun construction, resulting in short and choppy sentences. They often use key words again and again, making their writing sound repetitive.

Research shows that developing writing skills in grades 4-8 is best accomplished by providing many writing opportunities that emphasize a variety of styles. Student writers need to practice different sentence patterns. They need to learn how to move from simple subject/predicate forms to more complex sentence structures. They need to master the skills of sentence combining. Student writers also need to recognize various writing styles in the literature they read.

Contents

Using the Sentence Worksheets

While the lessons in this section are sequential, it is not necessary to teach this group of seven lessons as a unit. To keep your writing lab vital and maintain student interest, a more effective approach is to work on sentences at various times throughout the school year.

These sentence construction lessons should be used on an "as needed basis." Lessons 1-4, which develop more complex sentence constructions, may be used as instructional lessons with beginning writers whose sentence structure is short and choppy or used as review lessons with students whose writing demonstrates their ability to vary sentence structure. They may be omitted with students who have well-developed writing skills.

The sentence combining lessons may also be used on an "as needed" basis. Lesson 5 is instructional for students who do not understand sentence combining techniques. Lesson 6 uses

examples from student literature as a basis for sentence combining exercises. By writing in an author's style, students develop an idea of how successful writers use sentence variety to create a specific effect.

The last lesson in this section is a review of the sentence patterns taught in Lessons 1-4. It may be used in pre-/post- assessment of student achievement or used as a review of different sentence construction patterns. If not needed, it can be omitted.

Procedure

As students work on developing a variety of sentence patterns, you should follow these procedures:

- Be sure students are familiar with the various types of subject/predicate compounds before going on to work with compound sentences.
- Discuss ways different sentence patterns alter the meaning of the sentence.
- Encourage students to appreciate the contribution of sentence variety to an author's overall style.
- Point out that adding variety to sentence structure is often done in the revision stage.

Evaluation

Evaluation of lessons dealing with sentence construction is informal. Finished worksheets should be filed in students' writing folders. They may be used as reference guides for future writing activities.

Content Area Applications

Language Arts: revising previous drafts, expository essays, narratives, expressions of opinion, journal writing and responses to reading

Social Studies: reports, responses to reading, current event summaries and expressions of opinion

Name _____

Using Compound Subjects

Writers use a variety of sentence patterns to make their writing more interesting. When they put two sentence subjects together, we say the sentence has a compound subject. Writers use compound subjects when two people or things are doing the same action or have the same quality. Writing sentences with compound subjects helps keep your work from sounding choppy and repetitive.

Examples:

The football players were already on the field.

The coach was already on the field.

The football players and the coach were already on the field.

His trumpet is silver.

My flute is silver.

His trumpet and my flute are silver.

Superior intelligence is required for this job.

Organization skills are required for this job.

Superior intelligence and organization skills are required for this job.

1. **Draw a line** under the subject of each sentence in the last two examples.

2. Notice that when you make a compound subject, the subject of the sentence is plural. You may need to change the verb form slightly. **Draw a circle** around the verbs in the examples. Discuss the reasons for each verb change.

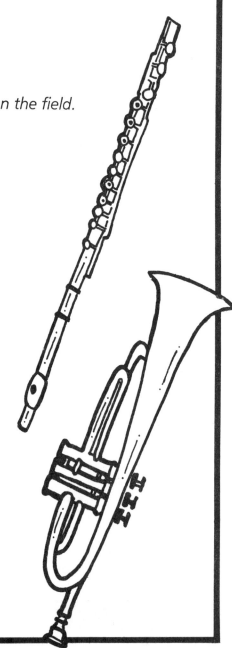

Work With A Partner

Underline the subject in each sentence. Combine the subjects and write one sentence with a compound subject.

1. Jimmy practiced skateboard tricks after school.
   John practiced skateboard tricks after school.

   _____

2. Cats are popular household pets.
   Dogs are popular household pets.

   _____

3. A singer must take lessons for many years.
   A pianist must take lessons for many years.

   _____

4. Agatha is often late to school.
   Harold is often late to school.

   _____

On Your Own

Write a compound subject that completes the following sentences.

1. _____ can wash a car very quickly.

2. _____ are my favorite television shows.

3. _____ are sports that require a lot of strength and endurance.

4. _____ are the latest fads.

Name _____

Using Compound Predicates

When writers put two sentence predicates together, we say the sentence has a compound predicate. Writers use compound predicates when the subject of the sentence is doing two different actions or has two different qualities. The single subject has two different predicates. Creating sentences with compound predicates can prevent written work from sounding choppy and repetitive.

Examples:

Those tourists <u>are sightseeing</u>.

Those tourists <u>are shopping for souvenirs.</u>

Those tourists <u>are sightseeing and shopping for souvenirs.</u>

Harold said he would mow the lawn now.

Harold said he would wash the car later.

Harold said he would mow the lawn now and wash the car later.

1. **Draw a line** under the predicate of each sentence in the last example.

2. Notice that when you make a compound predicate, the subject of the sentence does not change. You do not need to change the verb forms. **Draw a circle** around the verbs in the last example.

 **Work With A Partner**

Read the following sentences pairs. Underline the complete predicate in each sentence. Combine the predicates and write one sentence with a compound predicate.

1. I took off my soccer shoes.
   I cleaned off the cleats.

✏️➤ Work With A Partner ◂✏️

2. My cat likes to play with a yarn ball.
   My cat likes to chase her tail.

_____

_____

3. John finished his homework after school.
   John practiced skateboard tricks after school.

_____

_____

4. The clown tripped on his own feet.
   The clown fell over backwards.

_____

_____

✏️ On Your Own

Write compound predicates that complete the following sentences. Be sure each
compound predicate has two different verbs.

1. After school I have to _____

_____

2. On Saturdays I _____

_____

3. The long train _____

_____

4. The receptionist _____

_____

Name _____

Compound Sentences

Writers make compound sentences by joining two complete sentences. Each half of the new compound sentence has its own subject and predicate. In the examples below the subject and predicate are marked. The subject is underlined once and the predicate is underlined twice.

Examples:
The <u>teacher asked</u> for yard clean-up volunteers, and only two students <u>raised</u> their hands.

<u>Joanne wanted</u> red cheerleader outfits, but <u>Carol thought</u> they should be blue.

Compound sentences can be written in two ways. Whichever form is used, note that each half of the compound sentence has its own subject and predicate.

Using a comma

In one form the parts of the sentence are separated by a comma, and they are connected by a conjunction (and, but, or).

Examples:
George won first place in the high jump, and Bruce placed third in the broad jump.

My favorite ice cream is vanilla, but Dad likes chocolate much better.

Using a semicolon

Another way to write a compound sentence is to separate the parts of the sentence by a semicolon. In this form there is no conjunction.

Examples:
George won first place in the high jump; Bruce placed third in the broad jump.

My favorite ice cream is vanilla; Dad likes chocolate much better.

➤ Work With A Partner ⬅

Join the sentence pairs to make compound sentences. Use the suggested form.

1. The player kicked the ball toward the goalpost.
   The referee signaled a field goal. (conjunction)

   _____

2. The speedy rabbit thought he would win the race.
   The steady turtle came in first. (conjunction)

   _____

3. Put rough draft papers in the red tray.
   Randy will collect the final drafts. (semicolon)

   _____

On Your Own

Write a compound sentence that joins each pair of sentences. Vary the form and conjunctions used to connect the two sentences.

1. Mary gets to school on time every day.
   Bill is always late.

   _____

2. Fifth graders will sell hot dogs at the school carnival.
   Sixth graders will be in charge of the dunking booth.

   _____

3. We can go to the movies together.
   One of us can stay home and tape the basketball game.

   _____

4. Write your own compound sentence using either a conjunction or a semicolon.

   _____

Name _____

Compound Review

Analyze the following sentences. Identify each type of compound with these letters:

sub - compound subject
pred - compound predicate
sen - compound sentence

_____ 1. Alison planned her party well and sent out the invitations on time.

_____ 2. Steve's plane arrived on time, but no one was there to meet him.

_____ 3. The twins brought games on the trip; they entertained themselves all the way to Phoenix.

_____ 4. All the adults and students in the audience gave the cast a standing ovation.

_____ 5. Mr. Bradley sells auto insurance, and his son Brian wants to follow in his footsteps.

_____ 6. A good basketball player can change directions quickly and has good ball control.

7. Write a sentence with a compound subject. _____

_____

8. Write a sentence with a compound predicate. _____

_____

9. Write a compound sentence. _____

_____

Name_____

Using Other Sentence Patterns

Writers can make several sentence patterns by using words and phrases in a different order. This adds interest and variety to their writing style. Changing word order allows a writer to emphasize different ideas in the sentence without changing the basic meaning.

- **An adjective clause or two adjectives with a comma**
  The firefighters, who were strong and powerful, rushed into the blaze.

  Strong, powerful firefighters rushed into the blaze.

- **Parallel structure** (adjectives)
  Strong and powerful, the two firefighters rushed into the blaze.

- **An appositive**
  Harold, the strong powerful firefighter, rushed into the blaze.

- **A question or an exclamation**
  Who were the powerful firefighters that rushed into the blaze?

  Wow! The firefighters rushed into the blaze!

- **A prepositional phrase**
  Into the blaze rushed the strong, powerful firefighters.

- **Predicate noun or predicate adjective**
  The strong and powerful men were firefighters.

  The firefighters were strong and powerful.

- **Verb infinitive**
  To rush into the blaze is the job of firefighters.

- **A gerund phrase**
  Rushing into the blaze is dangerous, even for strong firefighters.

✏ Work With A Partner ✏

Use these ideas to write different sentence patterns. If needed, refer to the examples as a guide. Some sentence patterns work better than others with certain sentence ideas. When you are finished, put a check by the five sentences you think are the most effective patterns for this set of facts.

Stunt men are daring.
Stunt men are courageous.
The stunt men jumped out of the burning plane.
Scott is a stunt man.

An adjective clause _____

_____

Two adjectives with a comma _____

_____

Parallel structure (adjectives) _____

_____

An appositive _____

_____

A question _____

_____

An exclamation _____

_____

A prepositional phrase _____

_____

Predicate noun _____

_____

✏️→ **Work With A Partner** ←✏️

Predicate adjective _____

_____

Verb infinitive _____

_____

A gerund phrase _____

_____

✏️ On Your Own

Use these ideas to write five different sentences
patterns of your choice. Select the five patterns that
you think present the facts most effectively. Label each
pattern.

Runners are strong.
Runners are well-trained.
The runners raced around the Olympic track.
Joyce is a runner.

1. _____

_____

2. _____

_____

3. _____

_____

4. _____

_____

5. _____

_____

Name _____

Sentence Combining

Writers use sentence combining to create a more interesting writing style. Writers often experiment with several possibilities before selecting the most effective combination of ideas. As you read the examples, notice that some combinations present ideas clearly while other combinations are awkward and lack clarity.

Uncombined sentences

The truck was parked on the hill.
The truck is red.
The brakes on the truck failed.
The driver of the truck is in the cafe.

Combined sentences

1. The brakes on the red truck, parked on the hill, failed while the driver was in the cafe.

2. While the driver of the red truck sat in the cafe, the brakes on his red truck, which he had parked on the hill, failed.

3. The driver parked his red truck on the hill, but while he was in the cafe, its brakes failed.

Uncombined sentences

Harold wanted to play baseball.
He wanted to play on Saturday.
His friends were playing baseball.
They were playing in the vacant lot.
Harold's mother would not let him play.
It was starting to rain.

Combined sentences

1. Harold wanted to play baseball, but his mother wouldn't let him play in the vacant lot because it was raining on Saturday.

2. It was raining on Saturday when Harold wanted to play with his friends who were playing baseball in the vacant lot, but his mother wouldn't let him.

3. Saturday Harold wanted to play baseball in the vacant lot with his friends, but his mother wouldn't let him because it was raining.

✏️ Work With A Partner ✏️

Combine the following ideas into one sentence. Combine each set in at least two ways. When you are finished mark the combined sentence you think is most clearly written.

The train chugged over the bridge.
The train was pulled by an old locomotive engine.
The engine was puffing black smoke.
It was a suspension bridge.

1. _____

_____

2. _____

_____

Members of the orchestra watched the conductor.
Members of the orchestra were dressed in black.
The conductor raised his baton.
Members of the orchestra began to play.

1. _____

_____

2. _____

_____

Paige walked into the room.
The room was a mess.
The room belonged to her older brother.
Her brother had just left on a trip to Europe.

1. _____

_____

2. _____

_____

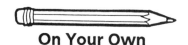

On Your Own

Combine the following ideas into one sentence. Combine each set in two different ways. Mark the combined sentence you think is most clearly written.

Peter stayed after school.
He stayed after school on Wednesday.
He was caught passing a note in class.
He was passing a note to Gabriel.
He was caught by Mr. Peers.

1. _____

_____

2. _____

_____

The rock star was young.
The rock star was handsome.
He ran up onto the stage.
He stepped into the spotlight.
The spotlight was red.

1. _____

_____

2. _____

_____

48

Name_____

Writing in an Author's Style

It is sometimes useful to use literature as a source for learning how to write more effectively. You can see how authors use language and sentence combining to add interest and variety to their writing style. You might want to try writing in an author's style. Sometimes, you may find that you prefer your own work to the original.

 **Work With A Partner**

The sentence-combining exercises on this page are taken from literature. Combine the author's ideas into one sentence. There are several possibilities for each exercise. Experiment with the possibilities until you find the one you think is most effective.

She was wearing a big fur thing.
The fur thing was yellowish-white.
She was wearing it around her shoulders.
She was carrying a plastic purse.
The purse was almost as big as a suitcase.
(*The Egypt Game*, Zilpha Snyder, p. 23)

_____

_____

_____

_____

_____

 **Work With A Partner**

He was a man of my father's age.
His beard was unkempt.
His hair was gray and sparse.
The lines of his cap were showing through his hair.
(*The White Mountains*, John Christopher, p. 22)

_____

_____

_____

He came right out of the trees.
He came right out of the falling snow.
He walked toward me.
He called my name.
(*Sing Down the Moon*, Scott O'Dell, p. 9)

_____

_____

_____

It was sunset.
It was a long day.
A stranger came strolling up the road.
He came from the village.
He paused at the Foster's gate.
(*Tuck Everlasting*, Natalie Babbitt, p. 17)

_____

_____

_____

_____

On Your Own

Combine these sentences from literature into one effective sentence.

Will was looking over a great forest.
The forest was white.
The forest was full of massive trees.
The trees were sturdy as towers.
The trees were ancient as rock.
(*The Dark is Rising*, Susan Cooper, p. 21)

_____

_____

_____

_____

I got down on the boards.
The boards were hot.
I was blinking my eyes again and again.
I was trying to lift the curtain of blackness.
(*The Cay*, Theodore Taylor, p. 47)

_____

_____

_____

_____

Meg looked into the crystal ball.
At first she looked with caution.
Then she looked with increasing eagerness.
She seemed to see an enormous sweep of dark and empty space.
Then she seemed to see galaxies swinging across it.
(*A Wrinkle in Time*, Madeleine L'Engle, p. 86)

_____

_____

_____

_____

Name _____

Sentence Patterns
Review

Write a sentence for each pattern. An example is given to help you.

Simple Sentences

1. subject/predicate — *The three girls were in the picture.*

_____

2. subject/predicate/direct object — *The spider caught a fly.*

_____

3. subject/predicate/direct object — *The policeman gave a ticket to the speeding driver.*

_____

4. subject/predicate/indirect object/direct object — *The policeman gave the speeding driver a ticket.*

_____

Compound Subject and Compound Predicate

Write two sentences for each pattern.

1. compound subject — *Boston and New York are located on the East Coast.*

_____

_____

2. compound predicate — *Jerry washes cars and mows lawns on the weekend.*

_____

_____

3. subject and subject/predicate and predicate — *Lifting weights and jogging build muscles and keep you in shape.*

_____

_____

Compound Sentences

1. compound sentence with a conjunction — *Martha has blue eyes, but her brother's eyes are brown.*

_____

_____

2. compound sentence with a semicolon — *Fifth graders are assigned to Mrs. Kelly in room 9; sixth graders should report to Mrs. Riley in room 11.*

_____

_____

Sentence Patterns

Write each of the following sentences in three different ways.

1. A strong, courageous lifeguard rushed into the sea to save a drowning swimmer.

_____

_____

_____

2. The slow and steady marathon runner crossed the finish line in first place.

_____

_____

_____

Paragraphs

Paragraphs - Expository Writing

Expository writing explains, analyzes, or persuades. The text is factual, reflecting the writer's understanding of content area learning, research, or the writer's opinion. Expository writing involves a logical sequence of ideas expressed in clear language. Expository writers effectively use paragraph organization and structure to help present concepts and information in an easy-to-understand format.

An expository paragraph is a group of sentences about one specific topic. One of the sentences (the topic sentence) states the most important idea about the topic. Other sentences support the main idea by giving more specific information about it. These sentences develop the main idea further with examples, evidence, or more specific details.

Writing Lab contains several basic frames that help students understand expository paragraph structure in order to develop an idea clearly. Student writers learn that while the number and order of sentences may differ, expository paragraph frames consist of three main things: a topic sentence, supporting sentences, and specific examples.

Contents

Lesson 1 - The Five Sentence Paragraph

Lesson 2 - The Power Paragraph

Lesson 3 - The Expanded Paragraph

Lesson 4 - Summary Paragraph - A simple book, like a Caldecott Award winner, is needed for this lesson.

Lesson 5 - Comparison Essays - This lesson is taught in 2 or 3 sessions.

Using the Paragraph Worksheets

The writing lessons in this section are sequential and should be used in the order they are presented. The paragraph frames build on the student's increasing understanding of how to use a topic sentence, supporting sentences, and elaborating details.

Follow these procedures when presenting the lessons:

- Work with the whole class in developing student understanding of each type of sentence used in an expository paragraph.

- Work with the whole class in developing understanding of each paragraph frame. If necessary, work as a group through the entire lesson.

- Discuss practical applications of expository writing.

Content Area Applications

Language Arts: summarizing main ideas, comparing/contrasting literary characters, themes, and settings, organizing information for oral presentation

Social Studies: research reports, responses to reading, explaining historical/political issues and events, comparing/contrasting historical/political issues and events, summarizing text information, letters to the editor.

Name _____

The Five-Sentence Paragraph

A paragraph is a group of sentences about one main idea. Each sentence in the paragraph gives the reader a specific piece of information. In a well-written paragraph, the sentences work together to develop the main idea.

When writers want to give several details about one main idea they will usually use three types of sentences. These are a topic sentence, supporting detail sentences, and a concluding sentence. The **topic sentence** introduces the main idea of the paragraph. **Supporting detail sentences** give more information about the main idea. The **concluding sentence** wraps up or summarizes the main idea.

Here is an example of a paragraph with a topic sentence (1), three supporting sentences (2) and one concluding sentence (3).

(1) The mountains are a wonderful place to spend a vacation. (2) I love the peace and quiet. (2) Mountains provide recreation activities for everyone. (2) A full week in the mountains gives me a chance to hike along rustic paths, see a variety of animals, and enjoy the spectacular scenery. (3) When it comes to choosing a vacation spot, mountains are my first choice.

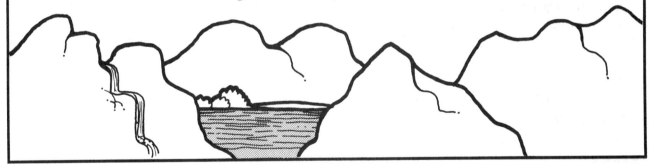

✏️ Work With A Partner ✏️

The five sentences in the following paragraph are out of order. Put the paragraph together in a logical sequence. Mark the topic sentence with (1), put a (2) by each supporting sentence, and write (3) in front of the concluding sentence. Rewrite the paragraph in the correct order on the back of this paper.

(   ) He spilled the red punch all over the white tablecloth. (   ) I was glad when it was over! (   ) His new toys sat on the floor while Bobby played with the ribbons and bows. (   ) Bobby's first birthday party was a disaster. (   ) Bobby's face was covered with cake and frosting.

On Your Own

Choose two of the following topic sentences. Use the five-sentence guide to write a paragraph for each of the following topic sentences. In the guide (1) is the topic sentence, (2) is a supporting sentence, and (3) is the concluding sentence.

Topic Sentences

Billy is a clumsy kid.

Looking back, I realized it had been a perfect day.

It was the most embarrassing moment in my life.

(Movie title) has everything it takes to be a hit.

It had been an exciting_____.

My friend _____ is a very special person.

(1) _____

(2) _____

(2) _____

(2) _____

(3) _____

(1) _____

(2) _____

(2) _____

(2) _____

(3) _____

Name _____

The Power Paragraph

A power paragraph is used to explain two or more facts about the main idea of the paragraph. Three main types of sentences are used to compose a power paragraph. The **topic sentence** tells the main idea of the paragraph. A **supporting sentence** states an important fact about the paragraph's main idea. An **example sentence** gives an example, evidence, or more specific detail about a supporting sentence. The sentences in a power paragraph are written in this order:

· topic sentence
· first supporting sentence
· example of first supporting sentence
· second supporting sentence
· example of second supporting sentence

Here is an example of a power paragraph. The topic sentence is marked (1), the supporting sentences are marked (2), and the example sentences are marked (3).

(1) The camel has adapted to its desert environment in two important ways. (2) First, the camel has a hump filled with fat. (3) The camel uses energy from the stored fat when there is not enough food to eat. (2) Secondly, the camel does a good job of saving water in its body. (3) The camel sweats very little even in the world's hottest deserts.

✏️ Work With A Partner ✏️

Number the types of sentences in the following paragraph. Mark the topic sentence with a 1, the supporting sentences with a 2, and the example sentences with a 3.

(   ) There are two enjoyable ways to spend a lazy Saturday afternoon. (   ) One way is to go to the beach and enjoy the fresh sea air. (   ) It is especially nice to stroll along the cool sand and search for shells. (   ) Another way to enjoy a free Saturday is to call a friend and go to a movie. (   ) Watching an adventure film while munching popcorn is high on my list of fun things to do.

⟨▭▭⟩ Work With A Partner ⟨▭▭⟩

Write a power paragraph using the following topic sentence. Begin each supporting sentence with a key word or phrase.

(1) There are two ways to avoid doing homework.

(2) _____

(3) _____

(2) _____

(3) _____

On Your Own

Choose a topic sentence from the list below. Write a paragraph using the 1,2,3,2,3 frame in which 1 is the topic sentence, 2 is a supporting sentence, and 3 is an example sentence. Use key words to point out the important ideas.

Topic Sentences

There are two important techniques to know about skateboarding.

The United States has two places every tourist should see.

Rain causes two problems.

The desert has two main features.

My teacher has two unusual qualities.

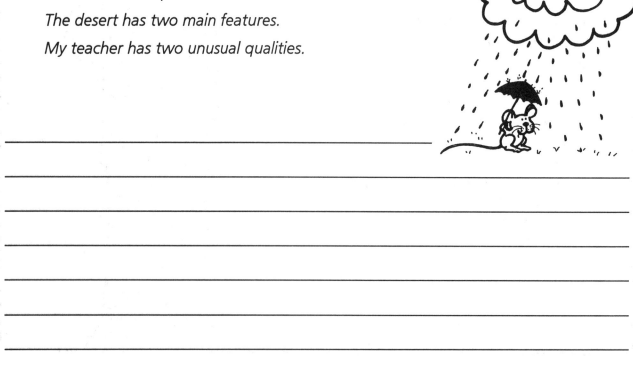

_____

_____

_____

_____

_____

_____

Name _____

The Expanded Paragraph

Some topics require longer paragraphs of eight or more sentences. The expanded paragraph is used to develop one main idea by using several supporting facts and examples. Four types of sentences are used in these paragraphs. These sentences are (1) a topic sentence, (2) supporting sentences, (3) example sentences, and (4) a concluding sentence. The sentences in an expanded paragraph are written in this order:

(1) topic sentence
(2) first supporting sentence
(3) example sentence(s)
(2) second supporting sentence
(3) example sentence(s)
(2) third supporting sentence
(3) example sentence(s)
(4) concluding sentence

Here is an example of a paragraph written using this order.

(1) The Statue of Liberty is a famous American attraction. (2) The Statue of Liberty stands on Liberty Island in New York Harbor. (3) It towers above incoming ships and seems to welcome them into the harbor. (2) In 1884 France gave the Statue of Liberty to the people of America. (3) The French wanted to thank Americans for helping them win freedom. (2) The statue is made of different metals. (3) Huge sheets of copper are hammered over an iron frame. (3) The copper gives the statue a bluish color. (4) Over the years, the Statue has become a symbol of American freedom.

 **Work With A Partner**

Number the types of sentences used in the following paragraph. Mark the topic sentence with a 1, each supporting sentence with a 2, each example sentence with a 3, and the concluding sentence with a 4.

( ) *The key to using the library card catalogue is knowing the three kinds of cards.* ( ) *Author cards are filed alphabetically by the author's name.* ( ) *To locate an author card, look under the first letter of the author's last name.* ( ) *Title cards are filed alphabetically by the first important word in the title.* ( ) *Ignore unimportant first words (the, and, an, etc.) in a book title.* ( ) *For example, the title card for* The Invisible Man *would be filed in the "I" section.* ( ) *Subject cards help you find books on a certain topic.* ( ) *Subject cards are easy to recognize because the subject is written in capital letters.* ( ) *Subject cards are particularly useful when you are doing a research project.* ( ) *When you understand how to use the card catalogue, you can find any book in the library.*

On Your Own

Use the following facts to write an expanded paragraph. Use the format 1-2-3-2-3-2-3-4, where 1 is a topic sentence, 2 is a supporting sentence, 3 is an example sentence, and 4 is a concluding sentence. Write your paragraph on the back of this piece of paper or on another piece of paper.

- There are many types of unusual spiders.
- Jumping spider - hunts its food, can jump more than forty times its body length, large eyes, short legs
- Dwarf spider - traps its food, spins a square web, lives near water
- Crab spider - looks like a crab, brightly colored, hides in flowers to catch butterflies and bees

Name _____

Summary Paragraph

The purpose of a summary is to explain a topic and its main supporting ideas. Only the most important information is presented. Details and examples are not included in a summary. The key to writing an effective summary is identifying the information to include.

The following example shows how other students practiced their summary writing skills. They used a simple fiction book, *The Greedy Zebra*. Their goal was to write only the main ideas. First they listened to the teacher read the first part of *The Greedy Zebra*. Then they wrote a summary of what they heard, using 25 words or less.

> *In Africa all the animals were dull and gray. One day a cave appeared with colorful furs. All the animals came except the greedy zebra. (25 words)*

Next the teacher finished reading the book. Then the students wrote another summary. This time, they summarized the whole story (including information contained in their first summary) in 25 words or less.

> *The dull animals found a cave of furs. Zebra got there last and found only black cloth. It split into stripes because of his chubbiness. (25 words)*

When they read each other's work, they may have found many differences in language and expression. Even though no two were alike, all the summaries gave the main ideas of the story.

⬅⬜ Work With A Partner ⬜➡

This page will give you practice in writing summaries. Use a simple fiction book. Listen to the story as it is read aloud. Use the set of lines to write a summary in 25 words or less. Write only one word on a line.

___	___	___	___	___
___	___	___	___	___
___	___	___	___	___
___	___	___	___	___
___	___	___	___	___

On Your Own

Use the grid below to summarize the following paragraph.

In the 1760s and 1770s, King George of England began passing laws about trade and taxes that the American colonists thought were unfair. When the colonists got angry, the king sent soldiers to control them. The colonists decided to fight for their freedom. They sent King George a Declaration of Independence. This important document listed their reasons for starting the Revolutionary War.

___	___	___	___
___	___	___	___
___	___	___	___
___	___	___	___
___	___	___	___

Name _____

Comparison Essays

Comparison essays point out similarities and differences between two or more things. Writers use different techniques to develop paragraphs for a compare/contrast essay than they use for other types of writing. Paragraph organization and writing style in these essays are designed to help the reader understand the purpose of the comparison. Each paragraph must do several things. It must develop more than one idea, follow a consistent sequence pattern, and fit as a logical part of the entire essay.

Writers develop a comparison essay in several stages. These stages are:

1. Write the thesis statement

First, the writer states the purpose of the comparison in a thesis statement. This important sentence identifies the two main ideas the writer is comparing. The thesis statement is the topic sentence of the essay.

2. Make a comparison chart

Next, the writer uses a chart to list supporting information for each main idea. The ideas in each section of the chart are ranked according to importance.

3. Choose an essay format

Then the writer chooses one of the essay frames shown in this exercise. By using the same comparison sequence in each paragraph, the writer helps the reader follow the development of supporting information for each main idea.

4. Write the essay

The writer uses the frame to write the essay. In the last sentence, the writer summarizes the thesis idea in a concluding statement.

 **Work With Your Class**

Use the following thesis statement for a comparison essay.

Thesis statement: *Cinderella and Snow White can be compared on three points.*

Use the chart below to list information for each point of comparison. When you have finished, analyze your list, looking for similarities and differences. Rank the ideas in order of importance. You need not use all the ideas listed on the chart when you write your essay.

Organization Chart for Compare/Contrast Essay

Cinderella   **Snow White**

family

_____   _____

_____   _____

_____   _____

problems

_____   _____

_____   _____

_____   _____

solutions

_____   _____

_____   _____

_____   _____

Two Models

Writers use special writing frames to compare or contrast two main ideas. Here are two models that are most usually used.

Model 1
The paragraphs in this frame are organized by supporting categories. Each main idea is discussed in the same sequence in each paragraph. An outline of this model would look like the following:

Thesis statement: *Cinderella and Snow White can be compared on three points.*

1. Family (topic sentence)
   - A. Cinderella
   - B. Snow White
2. Problems (topic sentence)
   - A. Cinderella
   - B. Snow White
3. Solutions/outcomes (topic sentence)
   - A. Cinderella
   - B. Snow White

Concluding statement

Model 2
The paragraphs in this frame are organized by the main idea. Each category is discussed in the same sequence in each paragraph. An outline of this model would look like the following:

Thesis statement: *Cinderella and Snow White can be compared on three points.*

1. Cinderella (topic sentence)
   - A. Family
   - B. Problems
   - C. Solutions/outcomes
2. Snow White (topic sentence)
   - A. Family
   - B. Problems
   - C. Solutions/outcomes

Concluding statement

Work With A Partner

Use your chart to complete the paragraph outline to compare Snow White and Cinderella using the first comparison model.

Thesis statement: *Cinderella and Snow White can be compared/contrasted on three points.*

Family (topic sentence) _____

_____

Cinderella _____

Snow White _____

Problems (topic sentence) _____

_____

Cinderella _____

Snow White _____

Solutions/outcomes (topic sentence) _____

_____

Cinderella _____

Snow White _____

Concluding statement _____

_____

_____

✏️ **Work With A Partner** ✏️

Use the paragraph outline to compare Cinderella and Snow White using the second model outline.

Thesis statement:
Cinderella and Snow White can be compared/contrasted on three points.

Cinderella (topic sentence) _____

_____

Family _____

Problems_____

Solutions/outcomes_____

Snow White (topic sentence) _____

_____

Family _____

Problems_____

Solutions/outcomes_____

Concluding statement _____

_____

_____

On Your Own

Use one of the outlines you completed for comparing Snow White and Cinderella to write a comparison essay by putting the information in paragraph form.

_____

_____

_____

_____

_____

_____

_____

_____

_____

_____

_____

_____

_____

_____

_____

_____

© Dandy Lion - Writing Lab

Descriptive Writing

Descriptive writing involves precise use of language. The writer becomes an illustrator, using words to create a visual picture in the mind of the reader. Descriptive writers work fluently and effectively with vocabulary, phrasing, elaboration, and figures of speech.

Developing Descriptive Writing Skills

There are two stages in helping students learn how to use descriptive writing. The first stage helps students distinguish between expository writing (writing that explains) and descriptive writing (writing that illustrates.) Developers of the California Writing Project refer to this distinction as the difference between "telling" and "showing." When comparing expository and descriptive writing samples on the same topic, students generally prefer the descriptive piece because they can visualize what the writer has said.

The second, more challenging stage enables students to incorporate techniques of descriptive writing into their own work. They learn to create pictures, moods and feelings through the use of descriptive adjectives and adverbs, imagery, simile and metaphor, personification and vivid details that appeal to the five senses.

Contents

Lesson 1 - Showing, Not Telling
Lesson 2 - Using Sensory Language
Lesson 3 - Figures of Speech
Lesson 4 - Writing Radio Advertisements

Using the Descriptive Writing Worksheets

The exercises in this section focus on techniques that help students acquire descriptive writing skills. The first lesson helps them develop a clear understanding of the characteristics of descriptive writing. The remaining lessons involve experimentation with vocabulary and elaboration. The descriptive writing lessons are not sequential; they may be used in any order.

When presenting lessons to your class, follow these procedures:

- Encourage students to discuss the purpose and possibilities of each assignment.
- Work with the whole class as you discuss the lesson examples. Ask, What technique(s) did the writer use? What effect(s) did the writer create? What other possible responses are there to the lesson example?
- Model the first activity on each worksheet by working through it together. Continue to work with students until you feel they are comfortable with the exercise.
- After whole-class presentations, have students work with a partner to discuss ideas, vocabulary, and techniques as they each write. Allow time for students to share their work with others in a larger learning group or with the entire class.

Evaluation

Evaluation of the descriptive writing lessons is informal. Ask each group to select the response they think is the most effective piece of descriptive writing. Read group models to the class. Discuss the characteristics of these student models. Ask, How does the writer use vocabulary? What other techniques does the writer use? Does the reader "see" what the writer has written? Finished worksheets should be placed in students' writing folders.

Content Area Applications

Language Arts: personal narratives, poetry, revising first drafts, responses to reading, reader's logs, reader's theatre

Social Studies: responses to reading, use of specific examples, elaboration of ideas, journal writing

Name _____

Showing, Not Telling

Writers have different purposes when they write. They can explain an idea so the reader understands it (telling). Or, they can describe an idea so the reader "sees" it (showing). Writers choose their words and style of writing to fit one of these purposes.

Examples

The sun rose in the east. **(telling)**

Blue-gray was slowly replaced by soft pink and then pure gold as the sun brought its light to the eastern sky. **(showing)**

The cute kitten played until she was so tired that she needed a nap. **(telling)**

The black and white kitten darted around the room, chasing the beam of light that was reflecting off the mirror. She rolled off the blue couch, bumped into the legs of the dining room chairs, and skidded across the polished oak floor. When I held the mirror still, she paused in a lion-crouch, preparing to attack the slippery light with a mad dash as soon as it reappeared. Her yellow eyes never left her target. Finally, when she was exhausted and her eyelids slowly began to droop, she folded her tiny white paws under her black chin, purred softly, and nodded off for an afternoon nap. **(showing)**

To "show" instead of just tell, writers use descriptive vocabulary and phrases that appeal to the five senses. They decide what they want the reader to see, hear, feel, taste, or smell. Then, the writers choose words and phrases to create the word picture that illustrates or shows the idea.

Work With A Partner

Change the following telling sentences into showing sentences. Add descriptive words and phrases that illustrate each idea. Discuss several possibilities before you write your response.

The theater was crowded.

_____

_____

_____

The kitchen was a mess!

_____

_____

_____

On Your Own

Choose three telling sentences from the list below. Use descriptive language to change them into showing sentences. Continue on the back of this paper if you need more room.

I could tell she was angry.	*It was a great picnic!*
The movie was exciting.	*The game was close.*
My bother/sister is such a pest!	*The house looked deserted.*
Litter was scattered everywhere.	*It was a colorful parade.*

1. _____

_____

2. _____

_____

3. _____

_____

Name _____

Using Sensory Language

Descriptive writing starts with a picture in the writer's mind. As he works, he chooses words that help the reader recreate the picture. He selects words with specific meanings. He uses nouns, adjectives, adverbs, and phrases that appeal to the five senses — sight, sound, touch, smell, and taste.

Here are some examples of sentences that have been rewritten to appeal to the senses.

The quarterback ran for a touchdown.

Weaving through the line of hulking defenders, the quarterback dashed over the green field and scored a touchdown.

The house smelled old.

As we entered the weather-beaten shack, we sniffed the musty odor created by years of accumulated dust.

✏️ Work With A Partner ✏️

Add more descriptive words to the list in each column. Continue on another piece of paper if you need more room.

Sight	**Sound**	**Touch**	**Smell**	**Taste**
blue	giggle	itch	floral	salty
glowing	clang	gritty	spicy	sour
blurred	coo	fluffy	perfume	savory
_____	_____	_____	_____	_____
_____	_____	_____	_____	_____
_____	_____	_____	_____	_____
_____	_____	_____	_____	_____

On Your Own

Write a description of an elephant for a person who has never seen one. You may not use any of the following words: *fat, obese, ears, trunk, wrinkled, husky, large, big, strong, tusks, gray or wild.*

_____

_____

_____

_____

_____

_____

_____

_____

_____

_____

What do you think a town called Bornski would be like? What would you see, hear, and smell there? Write a description that is so vivid that people who read your description will feel like they are actually standing in Bornski.

_____

_____

_____

_____

_____

Name _____

Figures of Speech

Writers use figures of speech to help the reader picture an idea in a different way. Figures of speech are words and phrases that have meanings that extend beyond their literal definitions. The four main figures of speech that writers employ are simile, metaphor, personification and imagery.

Simile - comparing two different things using the words "like" or "as."

> *The sun is like an orange ball, high in the sky.*

Metaphor - a comparison of two different things by making them seem equal.

> *The sun is an orange ball high in the sky.*

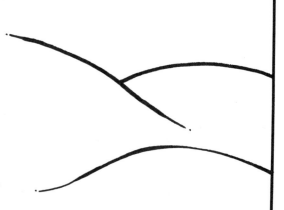

Personification - giving human qualities and abilities to objects or animals.

> *The wind moaned and cried through the night.*

Imagery - using descriptive words to create a strong sensation.

> *The empty room was completely bare; its rough wood floors and unpainted walls were cold enough to make us shiver to our bones.*

Identify these figures of speech by writing **S, M, P,** or **I** on the line.

_____1. Black clouds boiled and swirled in anger in the stormy night sky.

_____2. Her face brightened and her eyes twinkled like the stars.

_____3. As the salesman talked, the car hummed, coughed and finally died.

_____4. The lake was a mirror in the moonlight.

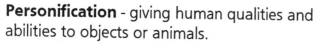

Answers: I, S, P, M

✏️ **Work With A Partner** ✏️

Figurative writing techniques are not limited to poetry, but are also found in prose. In the following sentences, identify each figure of speech by writing **S**, **M**, **P**, or **I** on the line.

_____ 1. She sat there smiling, a great sack of a woman with a round, plain face and calm brown eyes.

_____ 2. The sun was just opening its eyes in the eastern sky while the house rested in silence.

_____ 3. The slowly rising moon shimmered in the black night sky, while the lake, mirroring its silver reflection, lapped along the shore.

_____ 4. As he fell, his shoulders hit the ground like a ton of bricks.

Find examples from your reading text, from poems, or write your own examples for each of the following figures of speech.

simile _____

_____

metaphor _____

_____

personification _____

_____

imagery _____

_____

Answers: M, P, I, S

On Your Own

Complete the following sentences with figurative language. Your first idea may not be your most creative idea. Consider several possibilities before choosing an answer.

She was as thin as _____

They talked as fast as _____

The ants marched like _____

The tree looked like _____

Choose three of the following word pairs. Include each pair in a sentence that contains figurative language.

road - ribbon   dream - shadow
grass - carpet   garden - rainbow
kite - bird   football player - dancer

1. _____

_____

2. _____

_____

3. _____

Name_____

Writing Radio Advertisements

Radio messages depend entirely on language to create an image. Radio advertisements use descriptive words that appeal to the five senses. Advertising writers have to create a sensory image in the minds of the listeners.

Example:

Are you tired of dull, dingy, gray clothes? Do you have trouble telling your clean clothes and your dirty clothes apart? Do your friends think the grease spots on your shirts are polka-dots? Do your friends ask if your washing machine is broken?

Fabuclean will solve your laundry problems! Hard-working bubble action sends grease and grime away. White clothes sparkle! Colored clothes dazzle like a rainbow. One whiff of Fabuclean freshness and your nose knows the clothes are cleaner than new.

Run, don't walk, to your nearest store and carry home a box of Fabuclean today. Make your spotlessly clean clothes the envy of the neighborhood.

Reread the example. Underline the descriptive words and phrases that appeal to the listener's five senses.

 **Work With A Partner**

Select two of these topics. List some descriptive words and phrases that might describe the product or service.

Sudsey Wudsey Soap
Fun in the Sun Travel Tours
Miracle Green Plant Food
Munchy Crunchy Cereal
Jiffy Quick (fast food restaurant)
Chompers Dog Food

1. _____

_____

_____

2. _____

_____

_____

On Your Own

Use your ideas to write a radio advertisement for one of the topics. Remember to create a sensory image in the minds of your listeners.

_____

_____

_____

_____

_____

_____

_____

Persuasive Writing

Persuasive writing requires critical thinking and specific writing techniques. The writer's goal is to try to convince the reader to change his/her mind or take a specific action. Persuasive writers work with a logical sequence of ideas and specialized vocabulary in advocating a reasonable position on an issue.

Developing Persuasive Writing Skills

There are two stages in helping students develop effective persuasive writing skills. The first stage enables students to make the distinction between persuasion and threats or bribery.

Discuss the reasons people have for changing their minds — appeals to survival instinct, needs, wants, safety, intellect, financial gain or peer pressure. Working together, generate a list of powerful words used in persuasion — words like *ought, must, essential, necessary, best, powerful, economical* or *important.*

In the second stage of developing persuasive writing skills, students work with ideas and organization. This organization involves first developing a list of ideas that support the position. Next they evaluate the relative importance of each idea and then rank the ideas numerically, creating a logical sequence for presenting the argument. At this point, it is fairly easy for them to compose an introductory topic sentence and a conclusion that states the desired action. Lastly, they select the organization format for writing a persuasive paragraph.

Contents

Lesson 1 - Logical Reasons

Lesson 2 - Model 1 (Most Important to Least Important)

Lesson 3 - Model 2 (Least Important to Most Important)

Lesson 4 - Putting It All Together

Using the Persuasive Writing Worksheets

Writing lessons in this section are sequential and should be presented in the indicated order. The first lesson establishes the concept of persuasion by focusing on supporting ideas and specialized vocabulary. The second and third lessons help students organize ideas effectively into paragraph form. For best results, these lessons should be taught consecutively. In the fourth lesson students apply their persuasive writing skills in a short persuasive essay. When presenting these lessons, pay special attention to these instructional procedures:

- Encourage class discussion on practical applications of effective persuasive writing. Suggested applications might be job applications, politics, trials, sales presentations, consumer complaints or letters to the editor.
- Work with the class in developing reasonable supporting arguments for each topic. Remind students that good writing starts with having something to say.
- Discuss the importance of the introductory and concluding sentences in guiding the reader's thinking and action.
- Model each lesson by working with students until they demonstrate understanding of the thinking and writing techniques involved.
- Encourage students to look at supporting arguments on both sides of each topic before taking a position. Engage in a thorough discussion of ideas before ranking them. Allow interested students to propose their own topics for persuasive paragraphs.

Evaluation

Evaluation of the persuasive writing lessons is informal. Have each group write a brief summary of the techniques they learned in this series of lessons. Ask them to list two or three ways they will use their persuasive writing skills. Allow groups to share their ideas with the entire class. Finished worksheets should be placed in students' writing folders.

Content Area Applications

Language Arts: business letters, letters to the editor, job applications, public speaking, debate

Social Studies: responses to reading, understanding historical issues by writing from a first person point-of-view, evaluating controversial issues

Name _____

Logical Reasons

Persuasive writing has specific purposes. Writers who use persuasive writing want to:

1. convince the reader of an idea,
2. persuade the reader to take an action, or
3. change the reader's mind.

Writers persuade by giving the reader logical reasons to accept their point of view. The reasons may appeal to the reader's basic needs for food, shelter and safety or to the reader's desire for convenience, image, financial gain or entertainment. Writers may also appeal to the reader's intelligence or sense of fairness. Some writers persuade by appealing to the reader's desire to belong to a peer group. They use these appeals to give the reader reasons to take a specific action, use a certain product, or vote in a particular way. Certain words help writers persuade the reader. Some of the words they use are *ought, must, should, essential, necessary, need, important, concern, consequence, result* and *responsibility*.

Example

This is an example of something that is written with the intent to persuade.

There are three reasons why I think you should let me ride my bike to school. First, it would allow me to get to school earlier so I could work in the library as a library helper, a job I would really benefit from and enjoy. Secondly, I have a lot of books to carry to school, and it would be easier to carry them on the bike using a bike bag. Finally, I think I have shown that I am a responsible bike rider and bike owner. I ride legally and safely, and I take good care of my bike. Please give me your permission to ride my bike to school. It would be better than walking, and I have shown that I can handle the responsibility.

Underline the persuasive reasons used to convince the reader.

⬅️➡️ **Work With A Partner** ⬅️➡️

Write three logical reasons that will convince an adult reader to accept each of the following ideas.

1. Take a beach vacation instead of a mountain vacation

_____

_____

_____

2. Stop smoking

_____

_____

_____

3. Change a school rule or policy you disagree with

_____

_____

_____

4. Take back a defective product

_____

_____

_____

Review the reasons you and your partner wrote for each topic. Rank them in order from most important to least important by numbering them 1, 2, 3.

On Your Own

Select two situations from the following list. Write three logical reasons that will convince an adult reader to accept each of the ideas.

1. Allow you to have a new pet
2. Buy you a new pair of sports shoes
3. Buy candy you are selling for a school fund-raiser
4. Replace your bike that was stolen
5. Allow you to wear any hair style and clothes that you choose

Situation 1

_____

_____

_____

Situation 2

_____

_____

_____

Review your reasons for each topic. Rank them in order from most important to least important by numbering them 1, 2, 3.

Use the topic and reasons you developed in the first part of this lesson with your partner. Add example sentences for each reason you listed. Put all your ideas together. Write a persuasive paragraph that will convince an adult reader to accept your point of view.

Name_____

Most Important to Least Important

Persuasive writing needs to be well organized. First, the writer introduces the topic. Then, she presents her reasons in a logical order and gives examples to support each argument. Finally, the writer clearly tells the reader what conclusion(s) to draw or what action to take.

One effective technique of persuasive writing is to present reasons in order from most important to least important. A persuasive paragraph using this model would look like this:

Topic Sentence The topic sentence introduces the issue and states the position of the writer.

First reason State the strongest idea first, followed by an example sentence

Second reason State the second strongest idea, followed by an example sentence

Third reason State the weakest idea last, followed by an example sentence

Conclusion The concluding sentence states the attitude or action the writer wants the reader to take.

Here is a paragraph written using this most-important-to-least- important model. Note the use of transition words *first, second,* and *finally.* These words help the reader follow the writer's logical sequence of ideas.

(Topic sentence) There are three reasons I believe I should have an increase in my allowance. (Reason 1) In the first place, I have earned an increase by becoming more responsible. (Example) You have often thanked me for doing extra work around the house to help out. (Reason 2) Second, I use my allowance wisely. (Example) I have saved part of my allowance each week to buy some of my clothes, and they cost a lot. (Reason 3) Finally, I need more money. (Example) It's been a year and a half since I had an increase, and it costs more to do things now. (Concluding sentence) Please increase my allowance, because the amount I am asking for is reasonable and I have earned it.

✏️ ➤ **Work With A Partner** ◄ ✏️

Choose one of the following topics that were presented in Lesson One. Write an introductory sentence to introduce the topic and state your position. List three persuasive reasons for your position, in order from most important to least important.

1. Allow you to have a new pet
2. Buy you a new pair of sports shoes
3. Buy candy you are selling for a school fund-raiser
4. Replace your bike that was stolen
5. Allow you to wear any hair style and clothes that you choose

Introductory Sentence _____

Reason 1_____

Reason 2_____

Reason 3_____

Concluding sentence that tells the reader what attitude or action to take

_____

✏️ **On Your Own**

Use the topic and reasons you developed with your partner in the first part of this lesson. Add example sentences for each reason you listed. Put all your ideas together. Following the most-important-to-least-important model, write a persuasive paragraph that will convince an adult reader to accept your point of view. Continue on the back of this paper or on another piece of paper.

_____

_____

_____

_____

_____

Name_____

Least Important to Most Important

A persuasive writer who wants to take a more forceful position on a topic can vary the sequence of ideas. She can begin with the weakest idea and end with the strongest one. As a result, her ideas become more and more convincing as the argument develops.

This alternative technique of persuasive writing is to present reasons in order from least important to most important. The organization of a persuasive paragraph using this model looks like this:

Topic sentence   The topic sentence introduces the issue and states the position of the writer.

Third reason   State the weakest idea first, followed by an example sentence.

Second reason   State the second strongest idea, followed by an example sentence.

First reason   State the strongest idea last, followed by an example sentence.

Conclusion   The concluding sentence states the attitude or action the writer wants the reader to take.

Here is a paragraph written using this least-important-to-most-important model. Note the use of the transition words *first, second,* and *most importantly.* They help the reader follow the writer's logical sequence of ideas.

(Topic sentence) I would like a summer job at your company for three reasons. (Reason 3) First, I need something interesting to do with my time. (Example) Most of my friends are going away for the summer, and a job will give me a chance to spend my time doing something useful. (Reason 2) Second, I want to earn some money. (Example) Now that I am getting older, I have assumed the responsibility for more of my own personal expenses. (Reason 1) Most importantly, I will be an excellent employee. (Example) You can depend on me to be a responsible employee who will work hard for you. (Concluding sentence) I believe I am the best applicant for this job and hope you will hire me.

✏️➤ **Work With A Partner** ◀✏️

Choose a topic from one of the topics you used in Lesson One. Write an introductory sentence to introduce your topic and state your position. List your three persuasive reasons in order from least important to most important.

1. Allow you to have a new pet
2. Buy you a new pair of sports shoes
3. Buy candy you are selling for a school fund-raiser
4. Replace your bike that was stolen
5. Allow you to wear any hair style and clothes that you choose

Introductory sentence _____

3 _____

2 _____

1 _____

Concluding sentence that tells your reader the attitude or action to take _____

_____

_____

✏️ **On Your Own**

Use the topic and reasons you developed above. Add example sentences for each reason you listed. Following the least-important-to-most-important model, write a persuasive paragraph that will convince an adult reader to accept your point of view. If you need more room, continue on the back of this paper.

_____

_____

_____

_____

_____

_____

Name_____

Putting It All Together

In this exercise you will use your persuasive writing skills to support or oppose a student credit card. Read and discuss the facts given for the proposed student credit card. Look at both sides of the proposal before deciding your position on the issue.

The Facts

A local bank is offering a credit card for students. The requirements and restrictions for approval are:

· Minimum age is 12 years
· Credit limit is $100.00
· Minimum monthly payment is $10.00
· Applicant must have a savings account of at least $100.00
· Applicant must have a parent or guardian co-sign the application and be responsible for the debt if he/she defaults
· ATM card is included

Discuss the Issues

Work with a small group. Be sure you understand the requirements and restrictions for owning a student credit card. Ask your teacher to clarify any questions you have about the facts. Discuss the reasons you would like to have the card. Discuss possible problems that you might have if you owned a credit card.

 **Work With A Partner**

List the advantages and disadvantages of owning the credit card. Write your ideas on the organizational chart below.

Advantages   Disadvantages

_____   _____

_____   _____

_____   _____

_____   _____

_____   _____

On Your Own

Mark the three most convincing reasons for and against a student credit card. Number your reasons in order from most important (1) to least important (3) on each list. Take a position in favor of or against credit cards for students. List an example that supports your position for each reason.

1. _____

2. _____

3. _____

Put all your ideas together. On another piece of paper write a persuasive paragraph that will convince a reader to agree with your ideas. Follow either the least-important-to-most-important or most-important-to-least-important model of persuasive writing.

Revision

An Important Stage of Writing

Revision is one of the most important stages in the writing process. It is also one of the most difficult to teach. Consequently, meaningful revision of student work is often neglected or even omitted from the writing curriculum. The purpose of revision is to take a critical look at previous work and improve it. During the revision process, writing is made better or more effective.

There are two stages in helping student writers develop an understanding of the revision process. The first stage helps students recognize and value the positive effects revision has on their writing. Many students enter the middle grades (4-8) with the erroneous idea that writing a final draft consists of correcting spelling errors and copying the piece over in their best handwriting. This stage of instruction will let them see that there is more to this stage of writing.

Revision is an intrinsic part of *Writing Lab* lessons on clarity, sentences, paragraphs, descriptive writing and persuasive writing. Point out that when writers are elaborating meaning and developing a writing style, they are actually revising. As students begin to discuss their developmental writing lab exercises in these terms, they soon recognize that revision is at the heart of the writing process. Revision (with guidelines) is also emphasized in the section on modifying the writing process.

Secondly, students compare two drafts to see how a revised piece of writing is improved. They practice revision in a series of short exercises, each with a different focus. Finally, students work through a step-by-step revision lesson with a previously written piece of their own work.

Contents

Lesson 1 - Comparing Two Drafts
Lesson 2 - Revision Exercises
Lesson 3 - Guidelines for Revision (to be used as a reference for additional lessons)

Using the Revision Worksheets

The lessons in this section should be used after students are familiar with concepts and techniques taught in *Writing Lab* lessons on clarity, sentences, paragraphs, descriptive and persuasive writing. The revision lessons are sequential.

As you present revision lessons, pay attention to these things:

- Begin work on revision by reviewing Step 4 on "The Writing Process" reference sheet.
- Emphasize the importance of reworking (adding, deleting, reorganizing, clarifying or working on style) a piece of writing.
- Discuss the fact that techniques and strategies taught in previous lessons (clarity, elaboration, descriptive writing, vocabulary, sentence structure, organization) are used in the revision process.

Evaluation

Evaluation of the revision lessons is informal. Student responses will vary. Ask students to read their revised work to partners and group members. During class discussion, focus on effective written expression and improvement of the original piece of writing. Accept all work that shows application of revision strategies and techniques, demonstrates student understanding of the revision process, and is clearly written. Completed worksheets should be filed in students' writing folders.

Content Area Applications

Language Arts: revising previous drafts for full-process writing assignments in all domains, checking daily work for clarity and organization of ideas, developing a consistent writing style

Social Studies: revising full-process research reports, checking daily work for clarity and content organization, using specialized vocabulary

Name _____

Comparing Two Drafts

Revision is one of the most important stages in the writing process. When they revise, writers carefully reread their work. Revision offers them the opportunity to improve their work and make it more effective.

As they revise a draft, writers may do any or all of the following:

- use more synonyms, antonyms, and descriptive language
- clarify or restate unclear or awkward passages
- check to see if their purpose for writing is clearly stated
- elaborate or extend ideas by adding more details or examples
- delete repetitive words or passages
- rewrite or combine sentences to add interest and variety
- change the point of view
- reorganize ideas into paragraphs

 **Work With A Partner**

Compare the two descriptive writing drafts. Identify specific changes the author made in the revised piece. Look for changes in language, organization, and elaboration.

A Day at the Beach - First Draft

It was a special day at the beach. It was good to see the ocean again after such a long time. The waves were not very big as they came up to our toes. The sand was smooth, but here and there, a shell was sticking out. The sun was high in the sky, shining on the water. The birds were quietly resting nearby on a small ridge of rocks. Some seaweed had washed up nearby. Now and then a pelican flew down into the ocean trying to catch a fish. The cliffs at the end of the cove stood high above the water. Beautiful large beach houses were spread out along the top of the cliffs. I wished I could live in one of them so I would never have to leave this beautiful place.

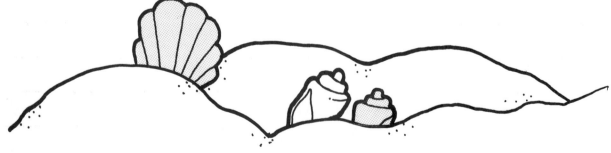

A Day at the Beach - Second Draft

Spending this special day at the beach was something I had looked forward to for a very long time. I was finally standing by the ocean again, in this peaceful, sheltered cove. The bright sun was high in the clear sky, its beams sparkling on the turquoise water. Shimmering white waves rolled up to the shore, tickling my toes with cool bubbles. Walking along in the smooth yellow sand, I spotted a mound that told me a shell was hidden there. Strands of seaweed had washed farther up onto the beach, looking like old frayed ropes that had been left behind long ago by careless sailors. As my eyes moved down the beach, they

rested on a flock of gulls quietly perched nearby on a small ridge of rocks. The birds looked like little guardians stationed at their posts, as they watched the waves roll in and back out. Now and then a pelican with its empty beak flew over, diving down into the ocean, trying to scoop up an unsuspecting fish. The cliff at the end of the cove stood high above the water. The winding old path to the top was barely visible through the jagged rocks and scraggly beach grass that clung to the side of the cliff. The large pink beach house was spread out along the top of the cliff, just as I remembered. I wished I could live in it so I would never have to leave this beautiful place.

Comparison Chart

Note changes that were made to the first draft of "A Day at the Beach" to produce the second draft.

_____

_____

_____

_____

_____

Name _____

Revision Exercises

On Your Own

The exercises in this lesson focus on specific areas of revision. Each exercise has one or more major flaws. As you read, think about the writer's purpose. Analyze the vocabulary, clarity, content organization, sentence structure, and use of elaboration. When you identify an area that is weak or incorrect, revise that part of the draft to improve the writing and make it more effective. Write a second draft of each exercise. Compare the changes you made with other students in your group.

The Meeting
(organization, variety, vocabulary)

The president called the meeting to order. "Today we need to decide how to spend the money we raised at the school carnival," he said.

"I think we should buy a new microphone," said Joanne.

"Why do we need that?" said Allison.

"I want to put mirrors in the classrooms," said Rosemary.

"No way, we need more P.E. equipment," said Eugene.

"I think we should take a poll of our classes before we decide," said the president. "The meeting is adjourned," said the president.

_____

_____

_____

_____

_____

_____

_____

_____

Astronomers

(repetitive vocabulary, sentence structure, clarity)

The astronomer wanted to see the stars. The astronomer took his telescope to the desert. The desert is a good place to see stars. The desert is good there because the air is clearly to see the stars better. Lots of people who are astronomers who want to see stars go to places where they can see the stars better.

_____

_____

_____

_____

_____

The Race

(clarity, referents, point-of-view)

Everyone knew the race would be between John and Mark. When the starting gun went off, John took the lead, but then he overtook him. By the middle turn he was only ahead by a few inches. As they came toward the tape, I burst into a sprint and won the race!

_____

_____

_____

_____

_____

_____

Trouble at the Tribune
(paragraph organization)

Tuesday was an exciting night in the newsroom. A raging fire had begun in a downtown high rise building. The computer system went out one hour before the deadline for the morning edition. The editor sent "Scoop" Johnson, his top reporter, to cover the blaze. Johnson was able to interview several victims who had been rescued from a fifth floor office. Technicians worked frantically to get the computer terminals back on line. The problem was solved when a short was found in the lead cable. He also spoke with an investigator about possible causes of the disastrous blaze. Johnson got his story in just before the deadline.

Name_____

Guidelines for Revising Your Work

Select something you wrote in an earlier exercise. Use these guidelines to revise the piece and develop a second draft. Make notes of the changes you want to make.

Revision Notes

Purpose of the writing _____

Content (additional ideas, deletions)_____

_____

_____

Sentence structure (completeness, variety of patterns, combinations)_____

_____

_____

Vocabulary (synonyms, variety, appropriate to purpose) _____

_____

_____

Paragraph organization _____

_____

_____

Clarity (awkward word order, sequence of ideas and phrases, point-of-view, omitted words, noun/pronoun and verb tense agreement) _____

_____

_____

Use your revision notes to improve your work. Write a second draft.

Modifying the Writing Process

Once student writers become experienced in the various stages of the writing process, modifications can be made that promote continued development of their writing skills. This is especially true of gifted and talented writers who are often verbally fluent and creative.

Traditional teaching methods used in the pre-writing stage of the process (clustering, outlining, written prompts) tend to produce drafts that are quite similar in both concept and content. Highly structured pre-writing activities can create a tight framework that may actually inhibit a creative or divergent approach to a writing assignment. The following lessons contain modifications that give students who understand the writing process freedom to select a divergent approach to the writing topic.

Pre-writing Activities

Oral pre-writing activities are based on reading, analyzing examples, examining various possibilities, and sharing ideas in a whole-class discussion. For these activities you should:

- Draw on shared personal experiences that relate to the suggested topic.
- Examine a wide variety of written or visual examples of the suggested topic.
- Read numerous examples of a genre, noting and discussing its distinguishing characteristics and specialized vocabulary.
- Discuss many possible applications of the suggested topic.
- Conduct whole-class discussions to establish the idea of the written piece.
- Give general guidelines for the writing assignment orally, allowing as much creative latitude as possible.

First drafts

A writer's first draft is produced by using fluent thinking. The purpose is to write ideas freely. A first draft is a creative effort built on the basic organizational structure of the assignment. At the first draft stage:

- Fluency is the objective.
- Many possible ideas are explored.
- Organization may be loose.

- Point of view is established.
- Spelling and mechanics are not relevant.
- Students should read and discuss rough drafts with a writing partner.
- Work is submitted for teacher comments and suggestions.

Revision

The revision stage is critical to excellent writing. The purpose of revision is to re-examine the piece for its purpose, content, organization, clarity, and style. **Teacher time spent on formative evaluation, during the revision stage results in significant improvement in students' writing on final drafts.** Comments written on student drafts should encourage students to evaluate, elaborate, restructure, clarify, and fine tune their writing. Teacher input and communication with students is most effective at this stage while the piece is still forming in the writer's mind. These guidelines apply to the revision stage:

- Rough drafts are submitted for teacher review.
- Comments, questions, suggestions for elaboration, organization or clarification, and praise for excellent use of language and phrasing should be written on the draft copies.
- Drafts are returned to students with a copy of writing guidelines, a writing checklist, and evaluation sheet.
- Students revise the work and write a second draft.
- A second teacher review is optional, depending on the nature of the assignment and quality of the first drafts.

When students' rough drafts are returned to them, they should also receive a copy of the writing guidelines, the writing checklist, and the evaluation sheet. The writing guidelines help students focus on revision strategies and provide an outline of things they will want to think about and possibly change when they write their final draft.

The writing checklist delineates correct writing points for content, style and structure, and mechanics and grammar. If a student has satisfactorily met a given criterion, a check mark is placed by the criterion. Points that are not checked tell the writer that this is something that needs to be changed. There is also an area on the checklist where you can write additional suggestions. The guidelines and checklist together give the writers a clear outline of what they need to change when they rewrite their pieces. The evaluation sheet is returned to the writer along with the rough draft and the guidelines and checklist. The evaluation sheet is distributed at this time so students will understand the criteria for evaluation. Students return the evaluation sheet with their final drafts. Final evaluation is made on this form. You may choose to check a grade and highlight certain phrases or you may write additional comments.

Teachers who spend the majority of their time in formative evaluation, guiding students through the revision process, find they spend much less time on final evaluation. Thus, teachers spend the same amount of time evaluating student work; the difference is when they spend it. In effect, the teacher and students are most actively involved at the same stages of the writing process.

Editing

The purpose of editing is to produce grammatically correct work. The procedures for this stage are:

- Students make corrections in spelling, mechanics, and agreement, using the checklist as a guide.
- Students may work with a peer editor.
- Beginning student writers may want to submit their final editing to the review of an adult reader.

Final drafts

Student work is submitted in its complete, final form. Presentation should include a cover (optional), title page, neatly written or typed body, any supplemental work or illustrations, and the evaluation sheet. Teacher evaluation consists of reading the written piece and marking the evaluation sheet. Teacher comments should highlight positive aspects of the student's work. Any shortcomings found in the final draft should be pointed out on the evaluation sheet rather than on the student's paper. Work at this final stage should meet the following criteria:

- Work should be error free, an example of the student's finest effort.
- Final drafts are submitted with the evaluation sheet included after the last page.
- All previous drafts are submitted separately at this time and later filed in writing folders.
- Final drafts are published or placed in students' writing portfolios.

Using the full process lessons

The three full-process lessons that follow encourage creativity and divergent approaches to a writing topic. Each lesson begins with oral activities and/or reading. Written criteria and guidelines for the assignments are distributed after students have submitted their first drafts. The format of the lessons is designed to maximize the amount of time students spend in revising their work and developing writing skills. The supporting worksheets and evaluation sheet that accompany each lesson assist teachers and students in formative evaluation during the revision process.

An A*B*C Story

This is a 26-sentence story or essay on any topic. Each sentence must start with a different letter of the alphabet used in consecutive alphabetical order.

Examples

Agatha washes her windows every weekend. Because she likes the sun streaming into her house, she feels it is worth the effort. Carefully she rubs bits of grime off the glass. Dirt that sticks is scraped off with a putty knife. Every now and then ...

Partially, but not completely mad, Joey sat down. Quickly eating his breakfast, Kirk said, "That was better than last time. "Right on!" Joey screamed.

Very noisily she scolded them one by one. When she was about to give everyone detention, the bell rang, the kids ran out, and school was dismissed. Xenopolis, the principal, later called Cathy to talk about the incident. "You think you've had a rough time," he lamented. "Zseesh!"

Since this lesson involves manipulation of language, students often use proper nouns (Quincy, Zelda; limit of two), exclamations (Zounds!), complex phrasing or sentence structure, and dialogue to solve difficult sequence problems. These problem-solving strategies should only be suggested by the teacher on an individual basis for students who have trouble with a section of their story. One revision is generally sufficient for this assignment.

Prewriting

- Present the concept, giving oral examples such as those shown above.
- Ask students to orally improvise several sentences that begin with sequential letters.
- Accept any appropriate content or story idea.
- Read examples aloud as models for student writing.

- Have students write rough drafts. They will generally solve the A*B*C problem during the rough draft stage.

Revision

- Assign partners for peer reading of rough drafts.
- Discuss drafts with the class. Discuss content, use of language, various solutions to the A*B*C problem, humor and story line.
- Do formative evaluation. Read all drafts. Write comments and questions that will guide students through the revision process.
- Read several examples of excellent writing as models for other students.
- Return drafts with guidelines, checklist and evaluation sheets.
- Have students write second drafts (optional).
- Peer editing and review with A*B*C Checklist.

Final drafts

- Final drafts should be presented with a cover and title page.
- Rough drafts should be submitted separately and filed in writing folders.
- Read and highlight positive aspects of the students' writing.
- Mark grades on evaluation sheets.

Publication suggestions

1. Reproduce stories in an anthology for parents.
2. Combine all originals and bind as one book to share with other classes.
3. Display final copies in the classroom.

A*B*C* Story Guidelines

Revising

The revision process includes a rethinking of the piece of writing.

- Once you have solved the problem of A*B*C in the first draft, work on your writing style. Vary the length and construction of your sentences. Try incorporating more prepositional phrases or descriptive language.
- Compare your draft to the suggested paragraph ideas. Make notes of areas that need more description, elaboration, or clarification.
- Develop the plot by elaborating with descriptive details that add to the humor or mood of your story.

Directions

Before you revise your story:

- Review the characteristics of the A*B*C* story.
- Review your sequence of events; be sure the narrative line contains a distinct beginning, middle, and end.
- Read the suggested paragraph ideas given in the next section.
- Be sure your point of view is consistently maintained.

Characteristics of an Effective A*B*C Story

A well-written story contains the following:

- a title
- a true or imaginary incident or sequence of events
- consistent point-of-view
- a specific time and setting
- a clear plot with a beginning, middle, and end
- twenty-six sentences, each beginning with consecutive letters of the alphabet
- only two proper names may be used to begin a sentence

Paragraph Ideas

The following paragraph ideas are suggestions only.

- **Opening paragraph** - Introduce plot events, characters, and ideas.
- **Middle paragraph(s)** - Continue to develop the sequence of events.
- **Ending paragraph** - Conclude the story with an ending that sums up the event described and possibly states the writer's feelings or response to the incident.

Give to students with their first drafts.

A*B*C* Story Writing Checklist

Name_____

A check means satisfactory work.

Content

_____ 1. Does the story have an appropriate title?

_____ 2. Does the story consist of 26 sentences, each beginning with a consecutive letter of the alphabet? Is each letter marked or underlined?

_____ 3. Does the writing consist of a logical sequence of events?

_____ 4. Does the sequence of events have a clearly developed beginning, middle, and ending?

_____ 5. Is the point of view consistently maintained?

_____ 6. Have only two proper names been used to begin sentences?

Style and Structure

_____ 7. Has descriptive language been used to elaborate and develop ideas?

_____ 8. Is the sentence structure varied?

_____ 9. Has the story been organized into paragraphs?

Mechanics, Punctuation, and Grammar

_____ 10. Have the rules for correct writing been followed?

_____ 11. Has dialogue been correctly written and punctuated?

_____ 12. Is there noun/verb and noun/pronoun agreement?

_____ 13. Are words spelled correctly?

Comments and Suggestions

_____

_____

A*B*C* Story Evaluation Sheet

Name _____

Title_____

_____**A** - The A*B*C* story begins with an appropriate title. This paper is a 26-sentence story; each sentence starts with a letter of the alphabet in correct sequence. The letters are highlighted to call attention to the pattern of the story. It contains a clearly developed sequence of events with a distinct beginning, middle, and end. The plot is based on a real or imaginary event. Time, setting, and point of view are established and consistently maintained. Character and plot are established using descriptive language and elaboration of ideas. Sentence length and construction are varied. Paragraph organization is appropriately used. The A*B*C* story follows the rules for good writing; there are no mechanical, grammatical, or spelling errors. The paper is neatly written or typed.

_____**B** - This paper contains most of the qualities of an A paper. It has a title, the pattern is correctly followed, and the letters are highlighted. The plot and characters are clearly presented, and a consistent point of view is maintained throughout the piece. The sequence of events has a beginning, middle, and end. Sentence construction, descriptive language, and style are apparent; however, these may not be developed as fully as the A paper. Paragraph organization is basically correct, but there may be some errors, especially in writing dialogue. The rules for good writing have been followed; however, there may be a need for more careful editing and proofreading.

_____**C** - This paper meets the minimum requirements of the assignment. The author writes from a consistent point of view. A sequence of events is presented, but it may lack clarity or elaboration. There is room for improvement in developing the content and style. There may be serious organizational flaws, especially in writing dialogue. The rules for good writing have been followed; however, there may be a need for more careful editing and proofreading.

_____**D** - This paper has serious flaws. It does not meet one or more of the criteria for an A*B*C* story.

_____**F** - Assignment not completed.

Essay on Childhood

This essay is based on an interview with the oldest person the writer can find. The essay will be a description of the subject's childhood, including family life, living conditions, cultural heritage, play, work, and education. Suggest that students talk with grandparents, relatives, neighbors, or family friends. Encourage them to interview a person older than their parents if possible.

Examples

These are samples of student writing on this assignment.

When she was eleven years old, Grandma Millie kissed her first boyfriend, Joe Singleton, behind a baseball backstop. She ran all the way home.
(Lawton Ziedses-des Plantes, grade 4)

He wore an old shirt and pants and a small jacket because it was cold in the morning. His shoes were old and had big holes, so they were just for the looks. For breakfast his mother cooked rice for him and his brothers and sisters . . . Because they were so poor, he drank a glass of water for lunch (they couldn't afford milk). He had rice for dinner at 4:00 p.m.
(Ellen Chen, grade 4)

I was so excited about my first paper cup, I squeezed all of the coffee out of it!!
(Jonathan Hoefs, grade 5)

When my grandma was twenty-five years old, World War II began (in Poland). During the war, she helped Jews who were hiding in her house. That's why she got a medal...and a tree in Jerusalem with her last name on it.
(Jan Kwiatowski, grade 5)

On Saturday night (Great-Aunt Ethel) often heard the street organ and went out to dance with it...Back then, girls wore aprons, blouses, and skirts. Boys wore trousers, a jacket, a hat and occasionally T-shirts. Usually my (Great) Aunt Ethel got her apron so dirty by Thursday (she started wearing it on Monday) that she couldn't wear it, so she had to borrow her mother's apron. She said kids were often dirty from mud and climbing into trucks, and kids did not have many clothes.
(Daniel Lenski, grade 4)

The war was terrible; most farms were destroyed and there was no food...My father's father went to war in South Korea in 1950. He was captured and hurt badly. He was a Korean P.O.W. But he managed to escape from capture and walked back to home for half a year begging for food at farms.
(Yujin Chung, Grade 4)

We traveled in a Ford. In those days, there weren't many cars but we were lucky enough to have one. It was black and instead of roll-up windows, it had snap-ons (today we'd call it plastic)...the car didn't move very fast, but of course twenty-five mph was pretty fast...in those days.
(Maia Taussig, grade 4)

Interviews

Since this essay is based on an interview, discuss the importance of preparing a list of questions before meeting with the subject. Questions should be open-ended and designed to elicit detailed answers rather than "yes/no" responses. For example, students could ask, "Can you describe how...?" or "What were your favorite...?"

Prewriting

- Present the concept, using photographs of children in a variety of activities and situations. An excellent source is *Life* magazine (Spring, 1990).

- Ask students to bring in family photographs of themselves or relatives that show something about their childhood (games, costumes, birthday parties, etc.).
- Share memories of your childhood by describing specific details of your daily life, games you played, chores around the house, leisure time activities, hobbies or favorite foods. Focus on ways your life was different from children's lives today.
- Encourage students to interview the oldest person in their family or neighborhood.
- Read several examples from the previous page aloud as models for student writing.
- Assign rough drafts.

Revision

- Assign or choose groups for peer reading of rough drafts. In learning groups, have students read a paper, pass it to the left, read another, continuing until a minimum of six to eight papers have been read. Ask each group to select one draft to be read aloud as a model.
- Conduct a class discussion of effective pieces of writing. Focus on detailed content and use of descriptive language.
- Provide formative evaluation. Read drafts. Write comments and questions on papers that will guide students through the revision process.
- Return drafts with guidelines, checklist and evaluation sheets.
- Assign second drafts. When these are submitted for teacher review, repeat the formative evaluation process.
- Allow for peer editing and review with the checklist.
- Assign final drafts.

Final drafts

- Final drafts should be presented with a cover and title page.
- Rough drafts should be submitted separately and filed in writing folders.
- Read and highlight positive aspects of the student's writing.
- Mark student grades on evaluation sheets.

Publication suggestions

1. Reproduce stories in an anthology for parents.
2. Combine all original work and bind into one book to share with other classes.
3. Display final copies in the classroom.

Give to students with their first drafts.

Childhood Interview Guidelines

Revising

The revision process includes a rethinking of what you have written.

- Analyze your writing style. Look for variety in sentence construction and descriptive vocabulary. Avoid slang and repeated words.
- Note areas that need further elaboration or clarification.
- Review the sequence of events to be sure it contains a distinct beginning, middle and end.
- Include very specific information that reveals details of the main character's life, personality or feelings.

Directions

Before you revise your interview:

- Review the characteristics of an effective essay listed below.
- Analyze your paragraph organization. Identify the main ideas.
- Be sure your first or third person point of view is consistently maintained.
- Be sure your verb tense is consistently maintained — present tense if using first person, past tense if using third person.

Characteristics of an Effective Childhood Interview

A well-written interview narrative contains the following:

- A title
- An introduction that identifies the character, time and setting
- A clearly developed sequence of events with a beginning, middle and end
- The character's personal feelings and reactions to the events in the narrative
- A conclusion that sums up the main ideas or gives the writer's reactions or opinions about the events or ideas.

Paragraph ideas

The paragraph ideas are suggestions only.

- **Opening paragraph** - Begin with an introduction of the main character. Establish the time, place, and any special circumstances that existed.
- **Middle paragraph(s)** - Develop a specific sequence of events, incidents or circumstances that help the reader get to know the main character. Develop the narrative with descriptive details. Be sure to include examples of the character's thoughts, feelings, or reactions as the sequence of events develops.
- **Ending paragraph** - End the narrative with a conclusion that includes your feelings or response to the interview and what you learned.

Childhood Interview Writing Checklist

Name _____

A check means satisfactory work.

Content

_____ 1. Does the writing relate events and details from the life of the main character?

_____ 2. Is first or third person point of view consistently maintained?

_____ 3. Is the time and setting clearly established?

_____ 4. Does the sequence of events have a clearly developed introduction, middle and conclusion?

_____ 5. Does the piece include feelings, thoughts or reactions of the main character that help the reader understand the character?

Style and Structure

_____ 6. Are ideas organized into paragraphs with a main idea, supporting information and specific examples?

_____ 7. Have sentences with similar words been combined?

_____ 8. Has descriptive language been used to elaborate and develop ideas?

_____ 9. Is the sentence structure varied?

Mechanics, Punctuation and Grammar

_____ 10. Has the rubric for correct writing been followed?

_____ 11. Is verb tense consistent?

_____ 12. Is there noun/verb and noun/pronoun agreement?

_____ 13. Are words spelled correctly?

Comments and suggestions

_____

_____

Return with first drafts and use for final evaluation.

Childhood Interview Evaluation Sheet

Name_____

Title _____

_____ **A** - This paper is clearly written, consisting of a well-developed sequence of events and details from the life of a person the writer has interviewed. Point of view is consistently maintained. The writer has established the time and setting using descriptive language and details. The essay has an introduction, body and conclusion that portray childhood memories of the subject. The feelings and thoughts of the subject are clearly communicated to the reader throughout the piece. Ideas and situations are elaborated to give the reader a visual picture of another time and place. The writer's perceptions and response to the interview may be shared in the conclusion. The paper follows the rules for good writing; there are no mechanical, grammatical or spelling errors. The paper is neatly written in cursive or typed.

_____ **B** - This paper contains most of the qualities of an A paper. The setting is established, and point of view is maintained throughout the piece. The information is organized and the essay has an introduction, body and conclusion. The piece includes the subject's personal feelings and reactions to the events; however, these may not be developed and elaborated as fully as in the A paper. The rules for good writing have been followed; however, there may be a need for more careful editing.

_____ **C** - This paper meets the minimum requirements of the assignment. The setting is established. The author writes from a consistent point of view. A sequence of events is presented, but it may lack clarity or elaboration. The author describes the subject's personal feelings or reactions in a general manner without using specific examples or descriptive language. The rules for good writing have been followed; however, there may be a need for more careful editing.

_____ **D** - This paper has serious flaws. It has not met one or more of the criteria necessary for an interview essay.

_____ **F** - Assignment not completed.

Tall Tale

This creative writing assignment is a personalized tall tale. The student writer selects characteristics of his/her own personality and real life events to exaggerate in a modern tall tale. Photographs of students in unusual situations or pictures taken from magazines serve as ideas for events in the tale.

This is an example of student writing (* marks a photograph or illustration).

> Many tales are told of Michael Nielsen, the prodigious explorer...Michael's special talents were recognized by those around him, and by the age of three, he was on his first assignment for the National Geographic Society. He was to review and interpret the social structure of the Zulus. His means of transportation to Zulu Land was via a handmade woven basket (*) which carried him down the crocodile infested waters...His friend, Louis Leakey, the anthropologist, was very impressed with Michael's work...(Later) he was to explore the Acropolis in Athens (*). His ability to speak Greek enabled him to add to the history of the Parthenon (*). He gave recommendations for the preservation of the ruins, but they were turned down. He single-handedly began to rebuild the Parthenon. (*) The local people were so appreciative of his efforts that they made him a king. (*) Later, they built him a throne. (*) (Michael Nielsen, grade 4)

Writing A Tall Tale

There are two stages involved in writing a tall tale. The first stage helps students develop a clear understanding of the characteristics of a tall tale. These popular stories stretch the truth and real-life conditions to extremes for humorous effect. Many tall tales reflect the hard work and pioneer spirit of America during the 1800s.

In understanding the tall tale format, students need to distinguish between exaggeration and fantasy. Reading numerous tall tales (Paul Bunyan, Pecos Bill, John Henry, etc.) helps them see how real life events, physical abilities, and personality traits are exaggerated. Paul Bunyan is an exaggerated character, not a magical one. His heroic feats are based on exaggeration of physical superiority and take place in the realistic world of lumberjacks. In the student example, Michael's ability to rebuild the Parthenon was based on his exaggerated intellect and physical superiority, not magical powers.

Once students are comfortable with the writing genre, the second step asks them to create tall tale characters that reflect aspects of their own personalities and lives. An excellent source of inspiration is photographs from a family album. Magazine or newspaper pictures are an acceptable substitute. For example, a picture of a youngster sitting in a wagon in front of a partially built house can become the basis for a tale about a successful developer, creating whole cities in a matter of days. A child posed on a statue of a bird, in the tall tale becomes a famous naturalist who travels around the country on her tamed eagle. Halloween and vacation photographs provide a wide variety of possible topics.

Prewriting

- Present the concept by having students read numerous examples of tall tales. Discuss the central characters and identify the exaggerated traits of each. Discuss the realistic settings of the tales.

- Discuss and list common characteristics of tall tales. Heroes have real occupations and perform monumental feats. In these stories heroes use exaggerated physical and mental traits and often the events are humorous.

- Look at a variety of photographs and pictures from a different point of view. Ask students to use imagination in exploring possible exaggerated interpretations of the visual prompts.

- Ask students to select one or more pictures as a basis for a personalized tall tale in which they are the central character.

- Encourage students to explore several possibilities of exaggeration in connection with their character. They may want to discuss their ideas with a partner before beginning to write.

- Read the student sample on the previous page aloud as a model for student writing.
- Assign rough drafts.
- Remind students that even though the writer is the hero(ine), the tall tale should be written in third person.

Revision

- Select groups for peer reading of rough drafts. In groups, have students read a paper, pass it to the left, read another, continuing until a minimum of six tall tale drafts have been read. Ask each group to select one draft to be read aloud as a model.
- Working with model papers, ask students to identify some of the characteristics that make these effective. Focus on exaggeration, humor, story line and use of descriptive language.
- Provide formative evaluation. Read drafts. Write comments and questions that will guide students through the revision process.
- Return drafts with guidelines, checklist and evaluation sheets.
- Assign second drafts. When these are submitted for teacher review, repeat the formative evaluation process.
- Peer editing and review with checklist.
- Assign final drafts.

Final drafts

- Final drafts should be presented with a cover and title page.
- Rough drafts should be submitted separately and filed in writing folders.
- Read and highlight positive aspects of the students' writing.
- Mark grades on evaluation sheets.

Publication suggestions

1. Write final tall tales on 2'x 3' lengths of colored bulletin board paper or poster board. Photographs and pictures should be attached throughout the text as they illustrate specific passages. Suspend two tall tales (back-to-back) from the ceiling or display them singly on classroom walls.
2. Reproduce stories in an anthology for parents.
3. Combine all original work and bind into one book to share with other classes.

Tall Tale Guidelines

Revision

The revision process includes a rethinking of the piece of writing.

- Compare your draft to the paragraph ideas given below. Make notes of areas that need further organization, elaboration or clarification.
- Check for use of exaggerated language, "show not tell" writing, descriptive adjectives and adverbs.

Directions

Before you revise your story:

- Review the characteristics of a tall tale.
- Be sure your tall tale illustrates a special quality or talent of the hero(ine).
- Review the sequence of events. The tall tale should be humorous and have a distinct beginning, middle and end.
- Be sure the third person point of view is consistently maintained.

Characteristics of an Effective Tall Tale

A well-written tall tale contains the following:

- a title
- one main character with exaggerated qualities, abilities or talents
- consistent third person point of view
- a clearly developed sequence of events with a beginning, middle and end in which the truth is stretched for a humorous effect
- a central character used to represent the best of his/her group
- exaggeration of real qualities or events that are shown by example rather than simply stated or supported by large numbers. A tall tale is rooted in reality rather than being a pure fantasy.

Paragraph ideas

The paragraph ideas are suggestions only.

- **Opening paragraph** - Begin the tale with a powerful topic sentence and supporting sentences that introduce and describe the character and his/her special traits.
- **Middle paragraph(s)** - Develop a specific sequence of events that illustrates the hero(ine)'s special abilities. Elaborate the episode with descriptive adjectives, adverbs, and language that add humor and exaggeration to the tall tale.
- **Ending paragraph** - End the tale with a strong conclusion that summarizes the special talents of the hero(ine).

Tall Tale Writing Checklist

Name_____

A check ✓ means satisfactory work.

Content

_____ 1. Are the exaggerated traits of the hero(ine) clearly established and described?

_____ 2. Does it include an exaggerated incident that happened to the central figure?

_____ 3. Does the sequence of events have a clearly developed beginning, middle and end?

_____ 4. Does the piece use exaggerated examples of reality to illustrate the hero's abilities rather than huge numbers or fantasy?

_____ 5. Is third person point of view consistently maintained?

Style and Structure

_____ 6. Have sentences with similar words been combined?

_____ 7. Have descriptive language, illustrative examples, and exaggeration been used to elaborate and develop ideas?

_____ 8. Is the sentence structure varied?

Mechanics, Punctuation and Grammar

_____ 9. Have the rules for correct writing been followed?

_____ 10. Is verb tense consistent?

_____ 11. Is there noun/verb and noun/pronoun agreement?

_____ 12. Are words spelled correctly?

Comments and Suggestions

_____

_____

Tall Tale Evaluation Sheet

Name _____

Title_____

_____**A** - This tall tale consists of a well-developed character description containing exaggerated personalty traits or abilities. It also contains a clearly developed sequence of events presented in chronological order that demonstrates the central character's exceptional abilities. The third person point of view is consistently maintained throughout the piece. The writer has established both character and plot using descriptive language and examples to illustrate special abilities instead of using just large numbers or fantasy. The writer uses humor and exaggeration. Ideas and situations are elaborated to give the reader a visual picture of the tall tale character and incident. The paper follows the rules for good writing; there are no mechanical, grammatical or spelling errors. The paper is neatly written or typed.

_____**B** - This paper contains most of the qualities of an A paper. The character is described and the third person point of view is maintained throughout the piece. The sequence of events is developed with a beginning, middle and end. The piece includes exaggeration and humor to illustrate the abilities of the hero(ine); however, these may not be developed as fully as in the A paper. The rules for good writing have been followed; however, there may be a need for more careful editing.

_____**C** - This paper meets the minimum requirements of the assignment. A sequence of events is presented, but it may lack clarity or elaboration. The author tells about the central character's abilities rather than illustrating them through exaggeration or specific examples. Large numbers or out-of-this-world fantasy may be used in place of exaggeration and humor. The rules for good writing have been followed; however, there may be a need for further editing and proofreading.

_____**D** - This paper has serious flaws. It has not met one or more of the criteria for a tall tale.

_____**F** - Assignment not completed.

Bibliography

Babbitt, Natalie. *Tuck Everlasting.* Toronto: Collins Publishers, 1975.

Cautrell, Paula and Kemppainen, Rick. *Purpose, Process, Product.* Bellflower: Bellflower Unified School District, 1990.

Christopher, John. *The White Mountains.* New York: Collier Books, a division of Macmillan Publishing Company, Inc., 1970.

Cooper, Susan. *The Dark is Rising.* New York: Scholastic Inc. by arrangement with Macmillan Publishing Company, Inc., 1973.

Hadithi, Mwenye. *The Greedy Zebra.* Boston: Little, Brown and Company, 1984.

L'Engle, Madeleine. *A Wrinkle in Time.* New York: Dell Publishing Company, Inc., 1962.

O'Dell, Scott. *Sing Down the Moon.* New York: Dell Publishing Company, 1970.

Olson, Carol Booth, ed. *Practical Ideas for Teaching Writing as a Process.* Sacramento: California State Department of Publications, 1987.

Snyder, Zilpha Keatley. *The Egypt Game.* New York: Dell Publishing Company, 1967.

Sparks, J.E. *Write for Power.* Los Angeles: Communication Associates, 1982.

Taylor, Theodore. *The Cay.* New York: Avon Books, a division of The Hearst Corporation, 1969.